GEOGRAPHY AND HISTORY

SECONDARY

BY ME

Cristina Granda Gallego
Raúl Núñez Heras
Simon Baskett
Belén Martín Alonso

PREHISTORY AND EARLY CIVILISATIONS

Contents

Getting started

0.1 Why we study History

History is a social science that studies mankind's past. Learning about the past involves finding out about the people who lived before us. To do this we must learn about what their society was like; what economic activities they had; what customs they held; how they thought; what they achieved; and also how they expressed themselves artistically.

By studying History, we can try to **explain** the main developments and events that took place in the past. This can also help us **understand** the political, social and economic situations of today.

Periods of History

To make studying History easier, we divide it into different periods.

The oldest period is the one that existed before the invention of writing: **Prehistory**.

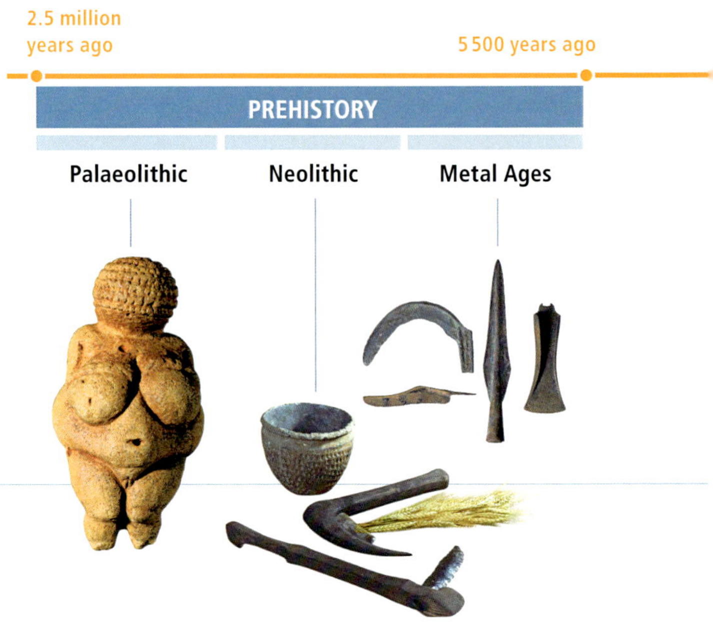

0.2 Historical sources

In order to study the past, historians must obtain information from a variety of sources.

Types of historical sources

Material sources: tools, buildings, weapons, jewellery, etc.	**Oral sources**: the accounts given by people who witnessed the events.
Written sources: books, inscriptions, letters, contracts, newspapers, etc.	**Visual and audiovisual sources**: photographs, videos, paintings, sculptures, etc.

At the same time, but in another place

When a particular historical event is taking place in one part of the world, something quite different may be happening elsewhere. So, in order to learn about History, we need to bear in mind the simultaneous nature of historical events.

The causes

In order to study a historical event, it is important to understand its causes. There may be several causes of any event and these causes may also be of different types, for example, economic, social, cultural, political, etc.

On the other hand, an event may affect another event, and may even become the cause of a subsequent historical event.

By studying the relationship between events, we can begin to understand the sequence in which historical events take place.

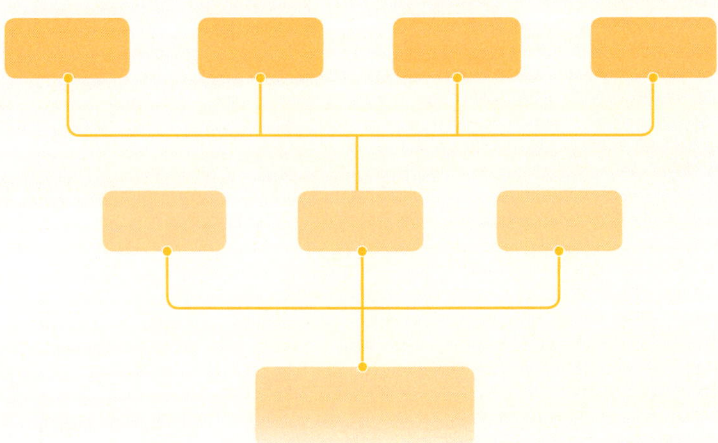

History is divided into four periods. The dates that mark the beginning and end of each period correspond to events that led to important changes.

Invention of writing 3500 BC	Fall of the Western Roman Empire AD 476	Columbus arrives in the Americas 1492	The French Revolution 1789

HISTORY

Ancient History	The Middle Ages	The Early Modern Period	The Late Modern Period

0.3 Putting historical facts in context

Every historical event takes place in a specific place and at a specific time. This is why **space and time** are essential to understanding History. Historians use **chronology** to put events in order in time, and they use different **units of time** to describe how long an event occurred for. The most basic units are:

year	365 days
lustrum	5 years
decade	10 years
century	100 years
millennium	1 000 years

There are also different ways of calculating historical time. In Western cultures, and in predominantly Christian countries, the most common are:

Before and after the birth of Christ	Before the present (years ago)
Dates before the birth of Christ are recorded in descending order. So, the higher the number, the earlier the year. For example, 2000 BC is about 4 000 years ago, and 3000 BC is about 5 000 years ago. These dates are written with the abbreviation BC (before Christ). For example, the Ancient Egyptian Empire began around 2686 BC. Dates after the birth of Christ are written in ascending order with the abbreviation AD (*Anno Domini*). This is placed before the number: AD 1492.	Sometimes historians choose to avoid using BC and AD. Instead, they refer to how many years have passed since a historical event took place. So, instead of saying 'writing first appeared around 3500 BC', we can say, 'writing first appeared about 5 500 years ago'. If you have a BC date and you want to say how long ago the event took place, you can add about 2 000 years to the BC date. This is because the current year is approximately 2 000 years after the birth of Christ.

01 Prehistory

<< LOOKING BACK

- What is History?
- Name the three main periods of Prehistory.
- What do archaeologists do?
- What marks the end of Prehistory and the beginning of History?
- What were the first tools made of?
- What is the difference between a nomadic life and a sedentary life?

4.5 million years ago
Australopithecus

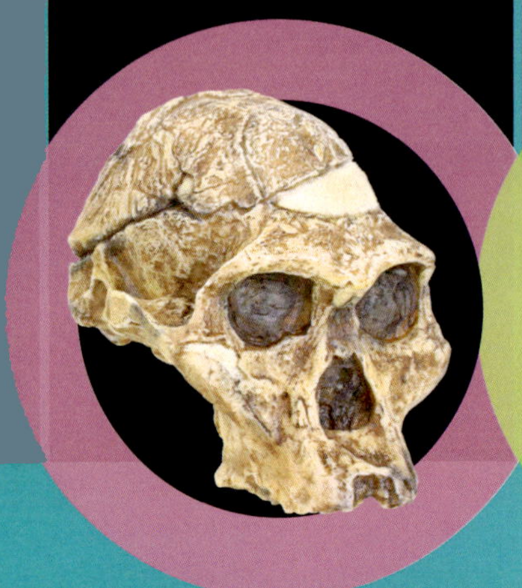

2.5 million years ago
Homo habilis

1.6 million years ago
Homo erectus

120 000 years ago
Homo neanderthalensis

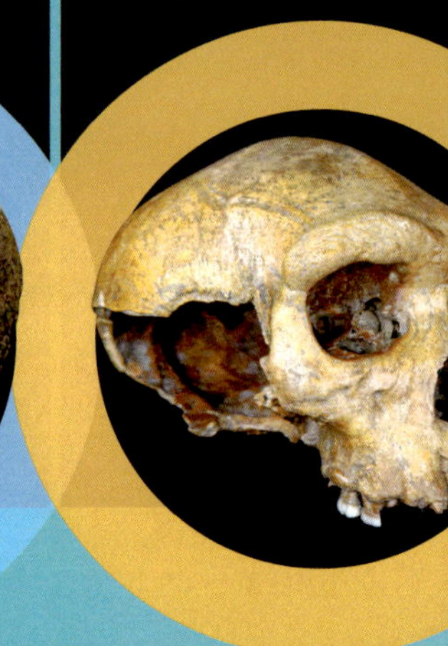

The skeleton and the Beatles song

In November 1974, in the baking heat of the northern Ethiopian desert, two palaeoanthropologists spotted a white object on the ground as they were walking back to their vehicle. They immediately recognised it as an arm bone belonging to a hominid (an early human being). Nearby they saw the back of a small skull and then a piece of a thigh bone. They eventually discovered 47 bones belonging to the same body.

After careful investigation they decided the skeleton was female. They named the skeleton 'Lucy' after the Beatles song *Lucy in the Sky with Diamonds,* which was playing on a tape recorder when the team were celebrating the discovery back at the camp.

Further investigations showed that Lucy was about 1.1 metres tall and weighed about 29 kg. She had a small brain, long arms and short legs – a bit like a chimpanzee – but she walked upright on two legs. Sophisticated technology used to date the skeleton estimated she lived about 3.2 million years ago.

Reconstruction of the hominid Lucy

- What is the name given to hominids that lived 3.2 million years ago?
- Where is Ethiopia located? What does this tell us about early human beings?

30 000 years ago
Homo sapiens

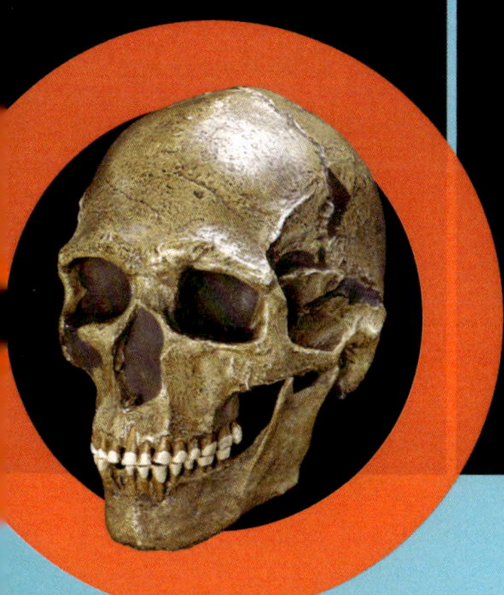

LOOKING FORWARD >>

- Do gorillas and humans have a common ancestor?
- Did Prehistory take place at the same time everywhere in the world?
- How did our ancestors live during the Palaeolithic period?
- What does the word *Neolithic* mean?
- What was the first metal used to make tools?
- Why did prehistoric people paint animals in caves?
- Where did the prehistoric inhabitants of the Islas Baleares bury their dead?
- What types of remains are found in archaeological digs?

1 Human evolution

Do gorillas and humans have a common ancestor?

Modern-day humans are the result of a **long evolutionary process** through which the human species adapted to its environment. Humans belong to the order Primates, which also includes gorillas and chimpanzees, and to the genus Homo. Over time, some primates **changed physically** and became different from the other primates:

- **Bipedalism:** They began to stand upright and walk on two feet. This meant that they could use their front extremities to make tools. They could also hold their head above their backs, so they became taller and could see further.
- **Opposable thumbs:** Hominids developed thumbs that could face and touch the other digits on the same hand. This meant that their hands were flexible enough to make tools.
- **Increased brain size** and **capacity**: Increased brain size made them more intelligent and enabled them to develop language and art.

The process by which these primates changed physically is called human evolution. It was a very slow process, during which some species coexisted. The only species that survived was *Homo sapiens*, to which modern-day humans belong.

These are the main species that underwent this process:

Richard Leakey was born in 1944. His parents, Louis and Mary, were famous palaeoanthropologists. His mother Mary was a member of the team that discovered Lucy. He left school at 16 after doing badly in his exams, but he went on to become a world famous fossil hunter and conservationist.
Do you remember what type of hominid Lucy was?

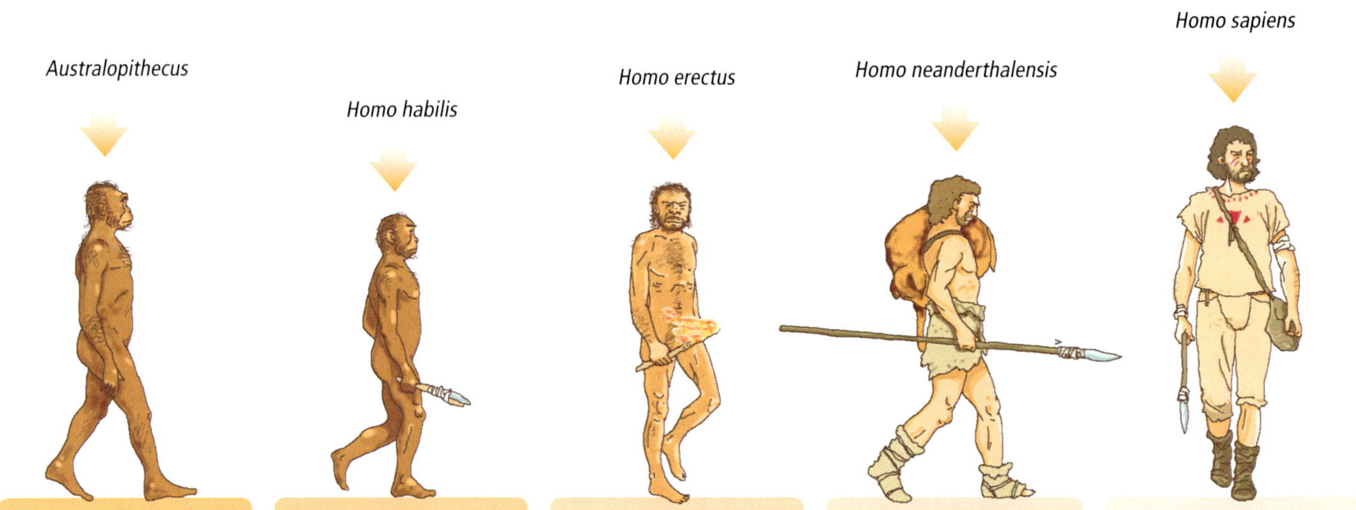

4.5–2.5m years ago. First bipedal primate.

2.5–1.6m years ago. First hominid to make stone tools.

1.6m–120 000 years ago. First hominid to use fire.

25 000–30 000 years ago. Coexisted with *Homo sapiens*, but died off.

From 200 000 years ago. The species that all humans belong to.

ACTIVITIES

1. Make a list of the physical changes that primates underwent during human evolution.
2. Make a short presentation to your class about the advantages and disadvantages of being a biped rather than a quadruped.
3. Richard Leakey's parents, Mary and Louis, were also famous palaeoanthropologists. Research one of them and write a short biography about him or her.

2 Prehistory

Did Prehistory take place at the same time everywhere in the world?

Prehistory is an extremely long period of time: it **begins with the appearance of the first humans**, over 2.5 million years ago in Africa, and **ends when humans began to write and make a record of their lives**, about 5 500 years ago.

Prehistory is divided into **periods of unequal lengths** which are determined by **advances in technology**. For example, when people started making tools from metal instead of stone, we move from the Stone Age to the Metal Ages. Also, these periods began at different times in different places, as you can see on this map:

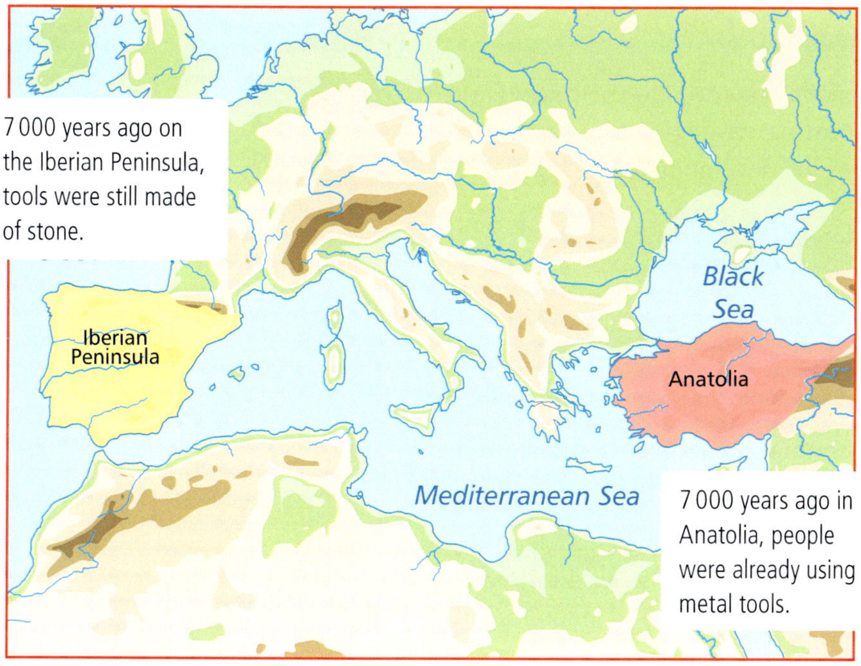

INVESTIGATING THE PAST

Prehistory is studied through archaeology. Archaeology is the study of material remains from the past. Thanks to finds such as fossils, tools and other objects, we are able to reconstruct the lives of our ancestors.

An archaeological dig

2.1 Periods of Prehistory

This table shows how Prehistory is divided up into ages, periods and sub-periods. The years shown are when each period began, not how long they lasted.

Age	Period	Sub-period	Beginning of period or sub-period
Stone Age	Palaeolithic period	Lower Palaeolithic	2 500 000 to 150 000 years ago
		Middle Palaeolithic	150 000 to 50 000 years ago
		Upper Palaeolithic	50 000 to 10 000 years ago
	Mesolithic period		10 000 to 9 000 years ago
	Neolithic period		9 000 to 7 000 years ago
Metal Ages	Copper Age*		7 000 to 5 000 years ago
	Bronze Age*		5 000 to 3 500 years ago
	Iron Age*		3 500 years ago

* Periods during which people had already begun to write and record their lives in some parts of the world (from 5 500 years ago)

ACTIVITIES

4. What event marks the transition from Prehistory to History?
5. What determines how we divide up periods of Prehistory?
6. Find out what you need to study at university to become an archaeologist. Do you think it would be a fun job? Discuss with the rest of your class.

3 The Palaeolithic period

How did our ancestors live during the Palaeolithic period?

The physical changes our ancestors underwent during human evolution enabled them to manufacture tools and weapons. These tools were made from stone, wood and bone. People began **carving stone** during the Palaeolithic period. In fact, the term *Palaeolithic* means 'old stone'. Stone tools became increasingly more effective and made it possible to hunt and cut up meat.

3.1 How people lived

During the Palaeolithic period, the way people lived varied greatly depending on the geographical area or climate in which they lived. However, we can identify a number of common characteristics:

- People **lived in small tribes**. Cooperation was essential to their survival. They protected each other, developed hunting strategies and passed on knowledge. These activities contributed to the development of language.
- They were **nomads**. They did not have permanent settlements and travelled around in search of food. They sheltered in caves and built temporary huts.
- They were **hunter-gatherers**. They did not know how to produce their own food. They gathered fruit, consumed carrion and hunted or fished.
- They **performed tasks as a group**. There may have been a division of labour between men and women. There was no private property.
- They **mastered fire**. They used it for heat and light, cooking, sending smoke signals, hunting and defending themselves against wild animals. Gathering around a fire helped build relationships and encouraged communication.

PALAEOLITHIC TOOLS AND WEAPONS

Hand axes began to be used during the Lower Palaeolithic

Carved stone arrow heads and the top of a wooden spear from the Lower Palaeolithic

ACTIVITIES

7. What does the word *Palaeolithic* mean?
8. Draw three stone tools or weapons and briefly describe how you would use them.
9. Work with a partner. Ask each other questions about the picture on the left. What characteristics of Palaeolithic life are shown?

4 The Neolithic period

What does the word *Neolithic* mean?

The Neolithic period **began about 9 000 years ago**, following a short transition period called the Mesolithic period. During the Neolithic period, humans went from being nomadic hunter-gatherers to sedentary **producers**. This change is also known as the **Neolithic Revolution**.

4.1 How life changed

During the Neolithic period, humans learned to produce their own food by farming the land and domesticating animals. **Agriculture** allowed humans to settle in one place and to abandon nomadic life. The result was the appearance of the first **villages**. These settlements were usually composed of huts and were located near rivers.

- **Societies became more complex and** hierarchical. Some settlements had leaders and other important people who managed resources.
- **New types of tools meant new types of jobs** came into existence. There was a **division of labour**, as different people performed different tasks.
- They **planted crops**, such as wheat and barley, and **domesticated animals**, such as goats, sheep and pigs. Food was more abundant and varied, so the **population grew**.
- People began to store and exchange surplus food, so **trade developed**.
- Archaeologists believe that **tasks were probably divided up between men and women**. Women were responsible for arable farming and making cloth and pottery. Men were responsible for livestock farming and manufacturing tools.
- Neolithic people had two main **religious practices**. They worshipped **the dead** and buried them with their possessions. They also worshipped **the forces of nature** in order to improve their harvests.

NEW STONE AXES

During the Neolithic period, stone was not only carved, but also polished. Stone tools were made smooth by rubbing them with another softer stone, such as sandstone.

A polished hand axe from the Neolithic period

ACTIVITIES

10. If *Palaeolithic* means 'old stone', what do you think *Neolithic* means?
11. List at least three differences between life during the Palaeolithic period and the Neolithic period.
12. Which period would you have preferred to live in: the Palaeolithic or the Neolithic? Discuss with your classmates.

4.2 Technological advances

New tools and objects were also developed during the Neolithic period:

In farming, **sickles** were used to cut crops and **hoes** were used to turn the earth.

Pots were made by hand and used to transport food and liquids.

Baskets were made of plant fibres to transport and store objects.

Later, people began to spin fibres and weave them with a **loom** to make cloth.

DID YOU KNOW?

Skulls from the Neolithic period have been discovered with holes drilled into them, suggesting that prehistoric people carried out surgical procedures on people's heads. Many of these holes had begun to heal before the person died, indicating that the patient survived the surgery.

Why do you think Neolithic people carried out this procedure?

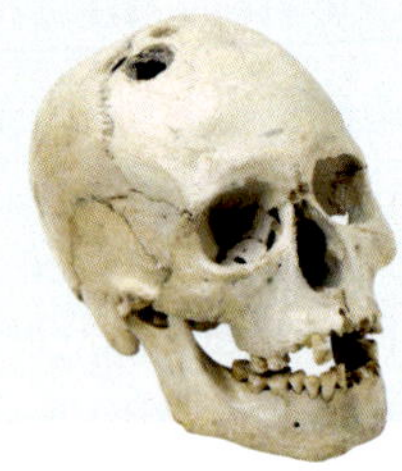

4.3 Origin and spread of the Neolithic Revolution

The Neolithic Revolution did not take place at the same time all over the world, although it did occur simultaneously in some areas. It began first in the Near East around 9000 BC, but only began in South America around 5500 BC.

ORIGIN AND SPREAD OF AGRICULTURE

Areas in which agriculture first appeared

- Agricultural areas in the Near East in the 8th millennium BC
- Spread of agriculture from the Near East
- Agricultural areas around the Indus River in the 5th millennium BC
- Spread of agriculture from the Indus River area
- Agricultural areas around the Hoang He River in the 5th millennium BC
- Spread of agriculture from the Hoang He River area
- Agricultural areas in the Andes in the 5th millennium BC
- Spread of agriculture from the Andes
- Agricultural areas in Central America in the 5th millennium BC
- Spread of agriculture from Central America

ACTIVITIES

13. Explain why people went from being nomadic to sedentary during the Neolithic period.

14. List some new tools developed during the Neolithic period and their functions.

5 The Metal Ages

What was the first metal used to make tools?

The Metal Ages is the name we give to the periods during which people began to **make objects and tools from metal**.

This brought about many **technological advances** which, in turn, brought about many **social and economic changes**. Copper was the first metal to be mined. It was used to make objects in the Fertile Crescent, in the modern-day Caucasus region.

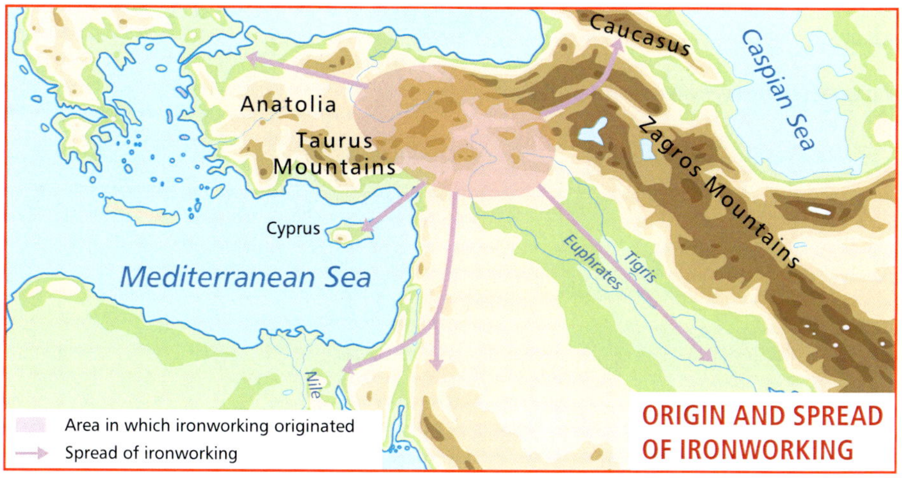

ORIGIN AND SPREAD OF IRONWORKING

DID YOU KNOW?

The Fertile Crescent region got its name for two reasons: in prehistoric times, the land there was fertile and good for growing crops, and when you see it on a map, it has the shape of a crescent moon. Where is the Fertile Crescent located?

5.1 Stages of the Metal Ages

The Metal Ages are divided into **three stages**:

THE COPPER AGE

- It began around 5000 BC in the Fertile Crescent area.
- Copper is a soft metal, which is easy to work into shape.

THE BRONZE AGE

- It began around 3000 BC in the Near East.
- Bronze is an alloy of copper and tin. This alloy is harder than copper. It was used to make stronger weapons and tools.

THE IRON AGE

- It began around 1200 BC in Anatolia.
- Iron is a harder metal than copper and bronze. It was used to make stronger and longer-lasting weapons and tools.

DID YOU KNOW?

In 1950, the mummified corpse of an Iron-Age man was discovered, preserved in a peat bog, in northern Denmark. The body was so well preserved that the people who discovered him thought that he had been killed recently! The mummy is known as the Tollund Man. Can you name an ancient civilisation that mummified its dead?

ACTIVITIES

15. Where was copper first used to make objects?
16. How do you think bronze was discovered? Compare your answer with your partner's.
17. What and where is the Near East? Find out which modern-day countries are in this region. Share your answers with your classmates.

5.2 Economic and social changes

- **New trade routes** were created as people travelled to find new sources of metal to make tools. This travelling helped spread different cultures.
- Trade produced **wealth** and **villages grew** significantly, giving rise to the first **cities**, which were often protected by defensive walls.
- There was a **specialisation of labour.** This meant that new types of professions, such as merchants and warriors, began to appear.
- Metal became a **symbol of wealth**, as people who owned metal weapons and tools were more powerful than those who had stone weapons. **War** became a means of expanding and controlling territory.
- **Private property** and **economic inequality** between people became more common. This meant that the structure of society became even more **hierarchical**.

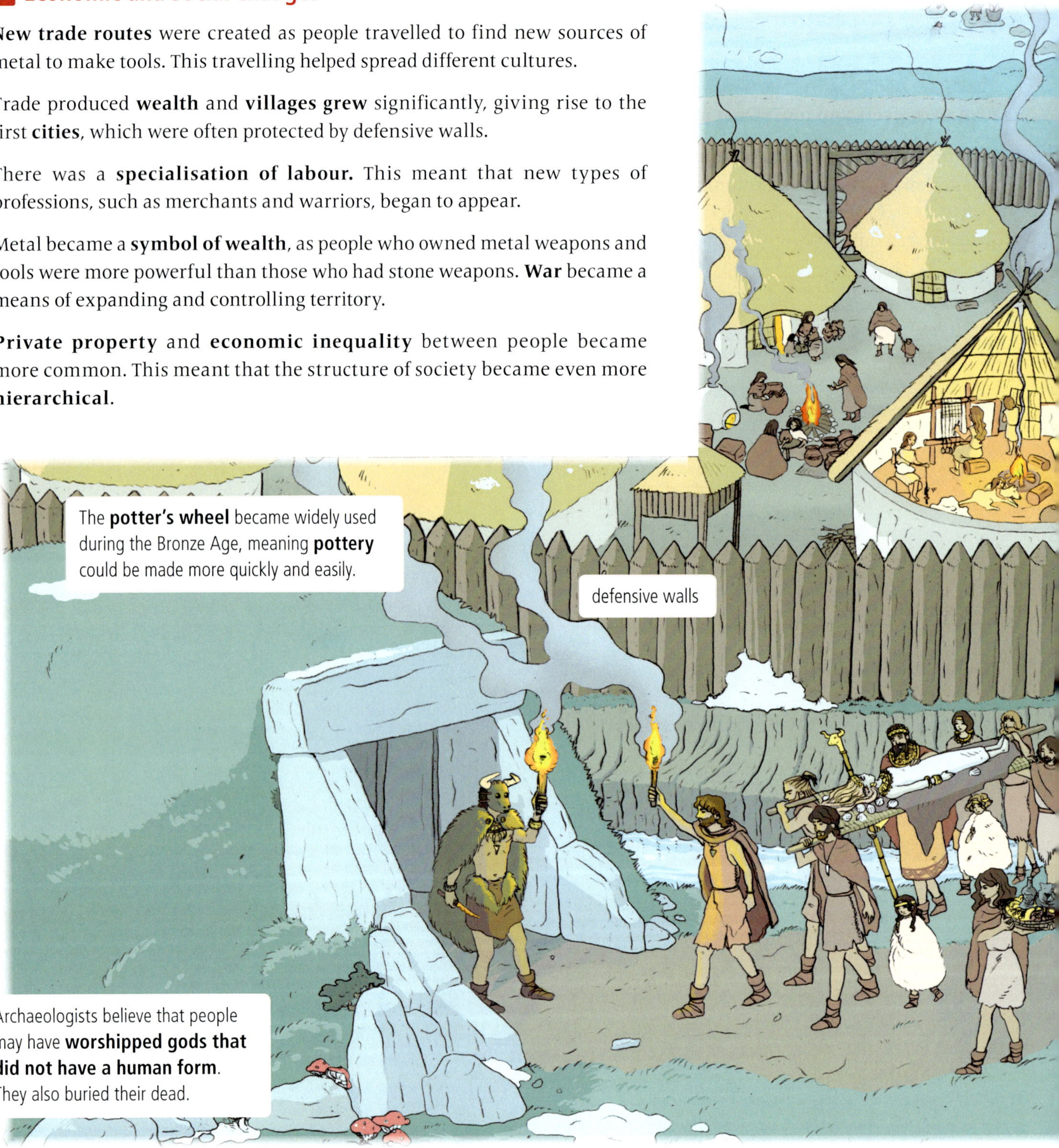

ACTIVITIES

18. Which materials were used to make huts during the Metal Ages?
19. Explain why metal was a symbol of wealth during the Metal Ages.
20. What was the main reason that society became more hierarchical during the Metal Ages?
21. Name two professions that appeared during the Metal Ages.

5.3 Technological advances

METALWORK

Most metals are extracted from an ore. People from the Metal Ages began to heat ore to separate the metal from it. This was called smelting. While the metal was still hot, it was put into a mould, then hammered into shape and finally polished.

NEW AGRICULTURAL TECHNOLOGY

In agriculture, wooden **ploughs** were replaced by metal ones, making it easier to turn and break up soil. The **sickle** was also improved, with metal blades replacing the stone ones which had previously been used.

22. Apart from making it easier to turn and break up soil, what other advantages would metal tools have over stone tools?
23. How do you think the invention of the wheel changed people's daily lives during the Metal Ages?

6 Prehistoric art

Why did prehistoric people paint animals in caves?

Prehistoric humans were concerned about many things in life: they were concerned about **obtaining food**, **reproducing** and **surviving the forces of nature**. They were also concerned about **death**. All of this is reflected in their art, religious practices and the way they buried their dead.

6.1 Palaeolithic art

We have found the remains of two types of artistic expression from this period: **cave paintings** and **portable art**.

CAVE PAINTINGS

Cave paintings were pictures produced on the **interior walls** of caves. The paintings were done with **pigments** obtained from a variety of different minerals. These pigments were mainly applied by hand. The figures were painted in several colours, especially ochre, red and black. Animals, such as bison, horses, deer and mammoths, were the most common **subjects** in these paintings. Many prehistorians believe the paintings had a religious meaning for the artists. For example, by painting the animals, the artists may have believed they would be easier to hunt.

The Altamira cave paintings (Cantabria, Spain)

PORTABLE ART

- Portable art consisted of carvings and **sculptures** that could be **moved from one place to another**. They were made of stone, bone or clay. Two types of figurines have been found:
- **Animal figurines**, such as horses and bison. These figurines were carved in bone or ivory and were primarily used as amulets.
- **Female figurines** which depicted the attributes of women. These figurines were carved in stone and are known as Venus figurines. They symbolised fertility.

The Venus of Willendorf (Austria)

A carved bison made of reindeer antler (La Madeleine, France)

ACTIVITIES

24. Are the following statements true or false? Correct the false statements.
    a. Prehistoric art depicted subjects which were of great importance to people.
    b. Only one colour was used in cave paintings.
    c. Venus figurines were portable pieces of art.
25. Explain the differences between portable art and cave paintings.
26. Find out more information about Venus figurines. Write a brief report about them. You can use the internet to help you.

6.2 Neolithic and Mesolithic art

There is not much evidence of portable art during the Mesolithic and Neolithic periods. Prehistorians believe that this was the result of people settling down and no longer requiring art that could be transported from one place to another.

Mesolithic and Neolithic art had the following characteristics:

- Paintings were done on stone surfaces in shelters or in shallow caves, but not inside deep caves. This is known as **rock painting**.
- The most common subjects of rock paintings were **hunting**, **gathering food** and **ceremonial dancing**.
- The figures were painted in a schematic **style**. They depicted essential features.
- The largest concentration of Mesolithic and Neolithic rock paintings in the world are found in the **east of the Iberian Peninsula**. They were usually painted in only one colour – normally black.

A hunting scene from La Valltorta caves in Castellón

6.3 Megalithic art

Megaliths are **monuments built using large stones**. They are the first known examples of architecture. They were created during the **Neolithic period** and the **Metal Ages**. Building these monuments required a lot of workers and a high level of organisation. Megalithic monuments can be classified as:

MENHIRS

- Large vertical stones embedded in the ground.
- They could stand alone or in a line with others.
- They were used for ceremonies.

DOLMENS

- A large, flat, horizontal stone laid on vertical stones.
- They were used as burial places.

STONE CIRCLES

- Several menhirs placed in a circle.
- They were used for ceremonies.

PASSAGE TOMBS

- Similar to a dolmen, but with one or more chambers and a passage at the entrance.
- They were used for burials.

ACTIVITIES

27. What were the most common subjects in rock paintings? How were these subjects depicted?

28. Find out information about the megalithic site at Stonehenge, England. What type of monument was built there? During which period was it built?

29. Work in groups. Discuss how you think megalithic monuments were built.
    - How were the workers organised?
    - Where did they get the stone from?
    - What tools did they use to put the stones in place?

7 Prehistory on the Iberian Peninsula

Where did the prehistoric inhabitants of the Islas Baleares bury their dead?

7.1 The first inhabitants

Much of what we know about the first inhabitants on the Iberian Peninsula comes from remains and artefacts found in the Sierra de **Atapuerca**, Burgos. The finds from Gran Dolina site at Atapuerca (see page 20) include human fossils and stone tools. These fossils have certain characteristics which are different from what we previously knew about the first inhabitants on the Iberian Peninsula. They belong to an 800 000-year-old hominid known as *Homo antecessor*.

Homo antecessor is believed by many scientists to be an ancestor of both Neanderthals and modern-day humans (although this is still being debated). Its height and proportions were similar to ours, although it was more heavily built and had a smaller brain.

7.2 The Palaeolithic and Mesolithic periods

Archaeologists have discovered many human and stone remains in different areas of the Iberian Peninsula, mostly in the north and east of the Peninsula. Some of the most well preserved prehistoric cave paintings in Europe are found on the Iberian Peninsula. These cave paintings are so well preserved because the caves are very deep and sheltered from climatic influences.

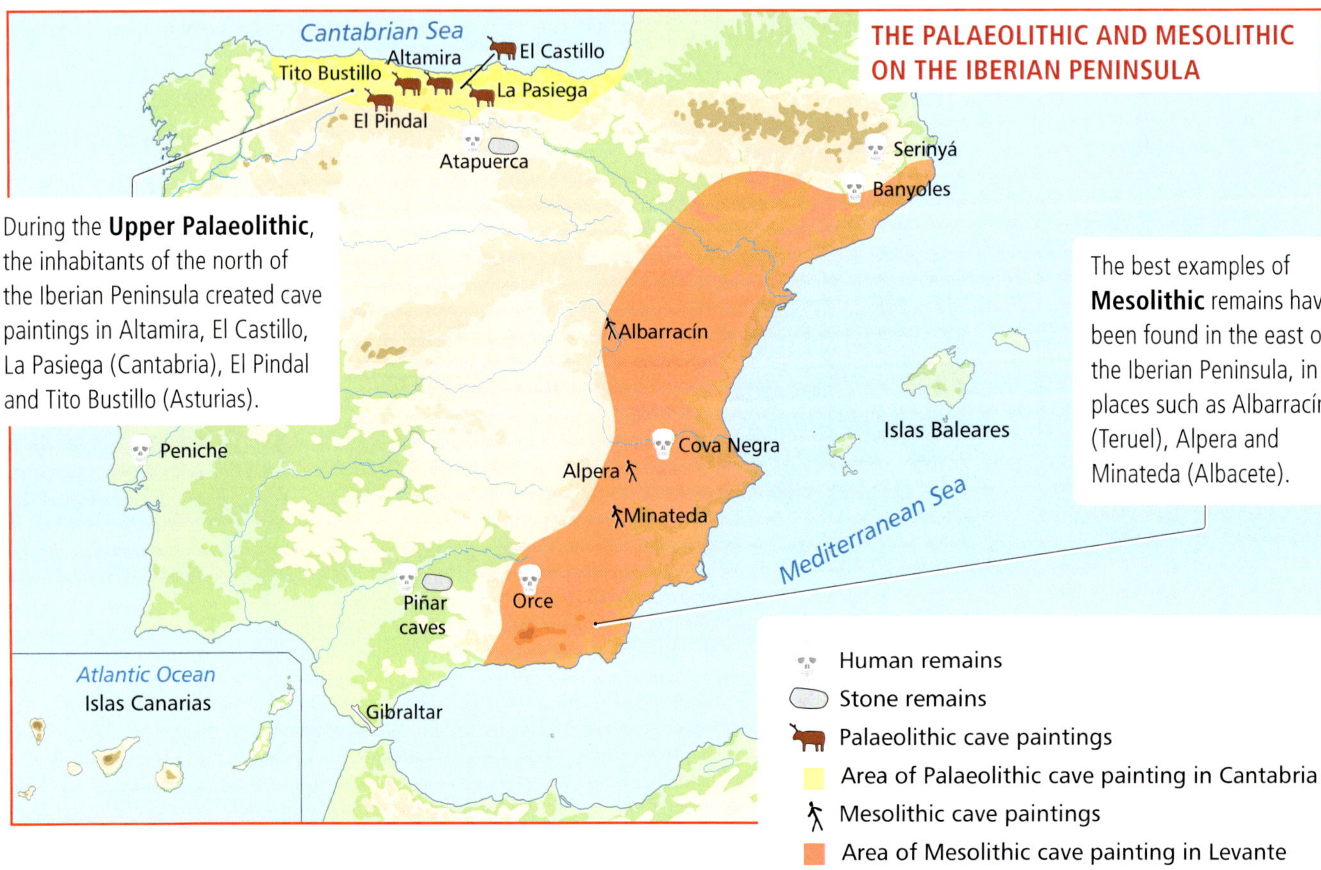

7.3 The Neolithic period and the Metal Ages

The technological advances of the Neolithic period reached the Iberian Peninsula via the Mediterranean more than 7 000 years ago. Metalwork began to spread on the Iberian Peninsula around 2500 BC. This technique flourished due to large deposits of copper and tin on the Peninsula. The main cultures which developed during these periods are shown below:

DOLMEN CULTURE

- It spread through the south of the Peninsula during the Copper Age.
- It was characterised by large megalithic monuments used for burying the dead.

CULTURE OF THE ISLAS BALEARES

- It began to spread during the Bronze Age.
- It was characterised by unique megalithic monuments, such as *taulas* (stone tables), *talayots* (watchtowers) and *navetas* (mass graves).

THE NEOLITHIC PERIOD AND THE METAL AGES ON THE IBERIAN PENINSULA

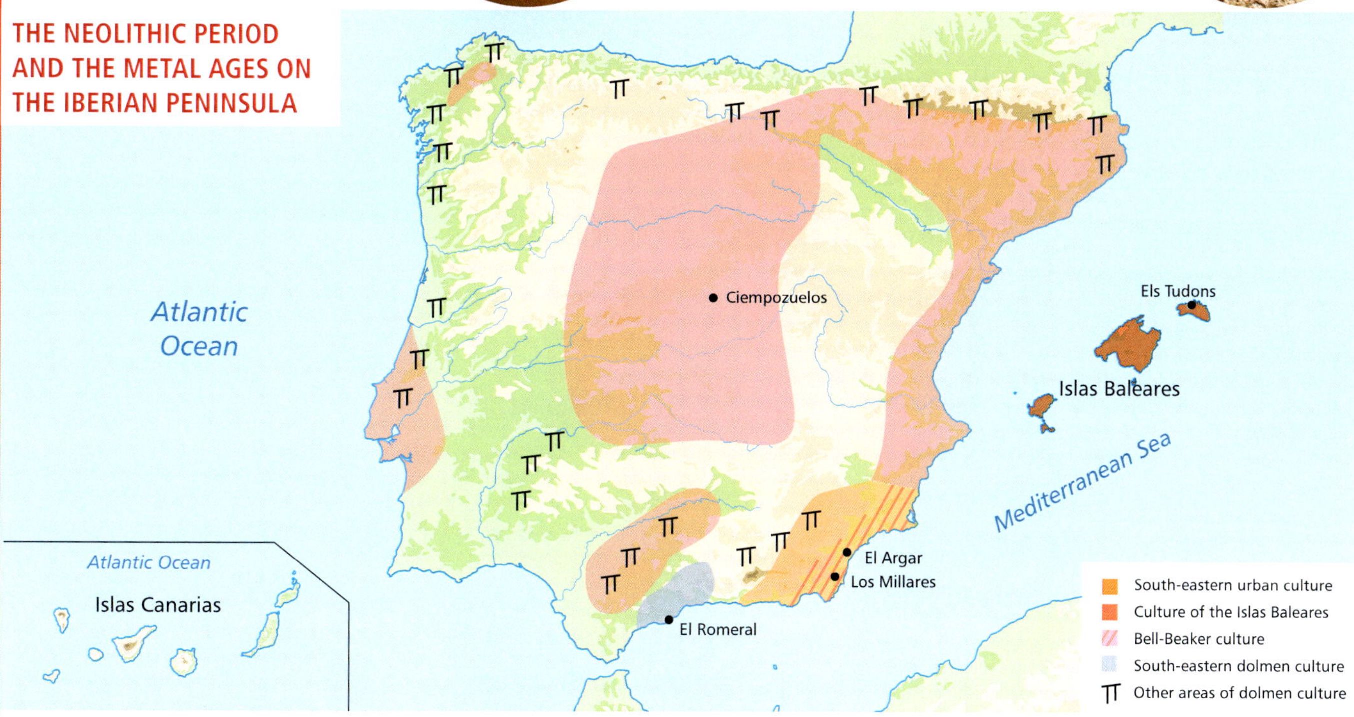

BELL-BEAKER CULTURE

- It originated in the south-eastern region of the Peninsula during the Copper Age.
- A bell beaker is a pottery container in the shape of an inverted bell.

SOUTH-EASTERN URBAN CULTURE

- It originated in the south during the Copper and Bronze ages.
- The walled settlement of Los Millares and the urban settlement of El Argar are notable examples of this culture.

ACTIVITIES

30. Correct these statements:

a. Human fossils and the remains of stone tools from the Palaeolithic period have been found at Atapuerca.

b. The Cave of Altamira contains remains of Neolithic cave paintings.

c. A bell beaker is a copper container in the shape of an inverted bell.

31. Look at the two maps of the Iberian Peninsula. The majority of the sites are located on or near the coast. Why do you think this is?

Discovery techniques

ARCHAEOLOGISTS AT WORK

In order to study the past, historians use lots of different historical sources to get the information they need, such as written, oral and visual sources. These historical sources are sometimes unavailable, as is the case in Prehistory. Therefore, historians must study material remains, such as artefacts and fossils, to try to piece together the past.

Archaeology is a branch of historical investigation which investigates material remains from the past. Thanks to the discovery of human fossils and everyday objects, such as tools and pottery, we can begin to understand how groups of humans lived in the past.

ARCHAEOLOGY AND PREHISTORY

Archaeologists study physical remains from the past. Their work is particularly important to the study of Prehistory, as there are no written records from that period. Therefore, all the information we have on prehistoric life comes from archaeology.

Types of remains found in archaeological digs

Structures

Structures, such as homes, monuments and public buildings often survive.

Artefacts

Artefacts can be everyday objects, such as tools, containers or ornaments.

Fossils

Fossils are the preserved remains of living things. The most common type is bones.

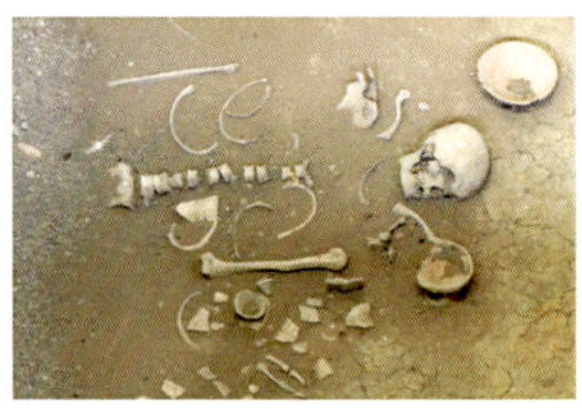

Stages of archaeological work

We can divide **the work of an archaeologist** into three stages:

1. Locate an archaeological site and carry out an excavation. During the excavation, archaeologists have to carefully plan all the tasks that need to be done and photograph everything they find in the exact place it was first discovered.
2. Carry out research on the site and examine the artefacts, fossils and other objects found within it. This research helps archaeologists to date the site and the objects, and to find out which historical period they belong to.
3. Make the information public by writing publications and reports on it, participating in conferences and presenting work at exhibitions and in museums.

1

2

3

What types of remains are found in archaeological digs?

The layers of an archaeological dig

Over time, sediment is deposited on top of the archaeological remains. Therefore, in archaeological digs, the deeper down the objects are found, the older they are, and the closer the objects are to the surface, the more recent they are.

ACTIVITIES

1. Imagine that you are part of a team of archaeologists and that you are excavating the site in the picture above. Apply each step of the archaeological process to carry out the activities below.
   a. Look at the images of the artefacts found at the site. Each one was found in a different layer of sediment in the dig. According to the periods of Prehistory you have studied, which layer would you find each one in?
   b. Once each object has been excavated from the site, each one is researched and dated. Organise the information you have about each object. Use the table of the periods of Prehistory on page 9 to help you. Make a fact file for each object, stating the material used to make it and the period of Prehistory that it comes from.
   c. Write a short report explaining how evolution allowed humans to make tools. Mention the physical changes that early humans underwent and explain how they helped them to make tools.

A

A carved stone tool

B

A polished stone tool

C

A bronze sword

Revision activities

1 Read the following text and answer the questions.

> “We humans are unusual creatures: we have no tail, we are bipeds and we have sinuous spines, long limbs, arched feet, agile hands and enormous brains. Our bodies are a mosaic of features shaped by human evolution over very long periods of time [...]. We can stand, walk, and run long distances with grace, but we suffer from sore feet and knee injuries. We can move and twist our spines, but most of us have back problems at some point in our lives. We can give birth to babies with big brains, but only through great pain and at great risk. For generations, scientists have tried to answer the question of how our bodies became the way they are. Now, using new methods from a variety of disciplines, they are discovering that many of the problems in our 'design' have a common theme: they are mainly caused by evolutionary changes that occurred when our ancestors stood upright – the first step in the long path to becoming human.”

ACKERMANN, J.
The Downside of Upright (adapted)
National Geographic, July 2006

a. Use a dictionary to find out what the words *sinuous*, *arched* and *agile* mean.
b. According to the text, what are the disadvantages of an upright posture?
c. What advantages does an upright posture offer humans? List other advantages you know of that are not mentioned.
d. Which physical features distinguish humans from other primates?
e. Find out who wrote the book *On the Origin of Species* and what the book is about.

2 Imagine you are an archaeologist who has just discovered the skull of an early hominid. Firstly, identify the hominid (use pages 6 and 7 to help you). Then, write a fact file about the hominid, including its name, when it lived and other information about it.

3 Put the following human advances in chronological order: *nomadism, permanent settlements, hunter-gatherers, stone tools, metalwork, the Neolithic Revolution, cave paintings.*

4 Use these sets of words to make full sentences about Prehistory:

a. sickles / cut / crops / turn / hoes / earth
b. stone / Neolithic period / carved / polished
c. surplus / store food / exchange / ability
d. mine / copper / metal / first
e. the Fertile Crescent / land / fertile / growing crops

5 Define the following terms: *History, Prehistory, human evolution, Stone Age, Metal Ages, nomad, sedentary, hierarchical society, worship, Fertile Crescent, Near East, loom, pottery, smelting, portable art, megalith.*

6 Look at the three photos of prehistoric axes below. Compare and contrast them. Which periods of Prehistory do you think they belong to?

A

B

C

7 Copy and complete the table in your notebook with the following terms (you may need to use some terms twice): *agriculture, carved stone tools, caves and huts, fire, first cities, first villages, hunter-gatherers, metal tools, nomads, polished stone tools, sedentary, the wheel.*

	Palaeolithic	Neolithic	Metal Ages
How they obtained food			
Lifestyle			
Where they lived			
Main inventions			

8 Answer the following questions:

a. Why did prehistoric people carve Venus figurines?
b. What is portable art? What period of Prehistory do you associate it with?
c. What are cave paintings? How are they different from rock paintings?

9 Put the following artistic artefacts in chronological order and state which period of Prehistory they belong to: *the stone circles at Stonehenge; the Venus of Willendorf; the cave paintings of Altamira; the cave paintings of La Valltorta.*

10 Look at the picture and answer the following questions.

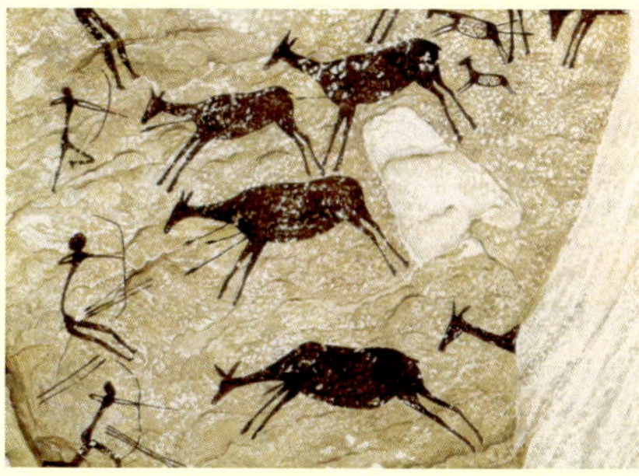

- What surface was this work of art painted on?
- What does it depict?
- What is its purpose?
- Is it realistic or schematic? Is there movement?
- Are the figures monochrome or polychrome?
- During what period of Prehistory was it painted?

11 Identify the following megalithic structures. Then, in your notebook, write a description of each one and explain what each one was used for.

A

B

C

D

12 Vere Gordon Childe was an Australian archaeologist best known for his theories about the development of prehistoric societies. He wrote the following text about the origin of hierarchical societies. Read it and then answer the questions.

“The Neolithic Revolution had other consequences apart from increasing the population [...]. The new economy allowed the farmer to produce more food than was needed every year to keep him and his family alive. In other words, it made possible the regular production of a surplus. [...] The surplus produced was insignificant at first, but it gradually increased until it demanded a reorganisation of society.”

Vere Gordon Childe
Excerpt from *The Urban Revolution* (adapted)

a. Explain one consequence of the Neolithic Revolution.

b. Explain the meaning of the word *surplus*.

c. In your opinion, what is the link between a surplus and the reorganisation of society? Think about: moving around, storage, diet, communities, division of labour, social hierarchy.

d. Imagine you are a Neolithic farmer. What crops would you grow? Would you keep any animals? How would you organise the division of labour in your Neolithic farm? Would you do the same activities all year round? Discuss with your partner.

13 Create a tourist information leaflet for a megalithic monument, providing information about its location, date of construction, type, use, etc. You can illustrate it with pictures, maps or drawings. You can choose one of the following megalithic sites or choose one yourself:

- Dolmen of Menga
- the Carnac Stones
- Stonehenge
- Naveta des Tudons
- the Moai on Easter Island

14 Imagine you are an archaeologist working on the archaeological dig at Atapuerca. Write a letter to your best friend. Include information about:

- the location of the dig
- any artefacts, fossils or other remains found
- the historical period these objects belong to
- what the artefacts were used for in the past
- what you enjoy most about being an archaeologist

You can use the internet or reference books to find out further information about Atapuerca and what has been found there.

Read and think

FOOD IN PREHISTORIC TIMES

The nomadic tribes of the Palaeolithic period were hunter-gatherers. The men of the tribe went out hunting while the women gathered **edible** roots, leaves, nuts, berries and small animals.

In the earliest 'hunts', about 2.5 million years ago, Palaeolithic men were only able to catch small **prey**, such as lizards, porcupines, tortoises, moles and insects. Over the next two million years, humans developed new hunting techniques. First, they killed larger animals by throwing rocks at them. Later, they made stone weapons, such as spears and arrows.

However, when hunters managed to kill larger animals, such as mammoths, two problems **arose** for the hunters. Firstly, how could they transport the meat back to their tribes and, secondly, how could they stop the meat from rotting? As Palaeolithic people had not yet learned to use salt to preserve food, the only solution was to live near the places where they hunted and collected food. Then, they ate as much of the food as they could as quickly as possible. They ate it raw because they had not yet discovered fire.

People who lived on the coast or near rivers and streams used to catch shellfish with their hands or make dams to trap small fish. They used wooden clubs or spears to catch larger fish, which also had to be eaten quickly because fish rots very quickly.

Then, about half a million years ago, people mastered fire. This meant that they were able to heat their caves, drive wild animals away and finally cook food. Experts believe that **roasting** was probably the first method of cooking and was probably discovered by accident – somebody probably dropped a piece of meat into the fire and waited until the fire died down before they could rescue the meat and eat it.

ACTIVITIES

1. Answer the questions:
   a. How was work divided up between men and women in the Palaeolithic period?
   b. How did the early hunters catch their prey?
   c. What problems did the hunters have when they killed larger animals? What was the solution?
   d. How did fire make prehistoric people's lives easier?
2. Find words in the text that mean the following: *collected; animals hunted for food; going bad; not cooked; big heavy sticks.*
3. How did stone tools make people's lives easier? What could they use them for?
4. Work in small groups. Imagine you are members of a Palaeolithic tribe. You and other tribespeople have come back to your cave after a long day of hunting and gathering, and you meet around the fire. Explain what you have hunted or gathered and decide what you are going to have for supper. You can use your dictionaries or the internet to find the names of any plants or animals that you do not know in English.

Work it out

CONCEPT MAP

Use the words in the word cloud to create your own unit map in your notebook. Write any connecting texts you need.

Palaeolithic period · agriculture · hunter-gatherers · mastered fire · huts · hierarchical society · caves · villages · nomads · **Prehistory** · Neolithic period · Metal Ages · sedentary producers · metalworking · cities · carved stone · polished stone

SELF-ASSESSMENT

Carry out a self-assessment of what you have learnt in this unit. Choose one answer for each question and then check your answers.

1. The ... is the earliest and longest period of Prehistory.
   a. Palaeolithic period
   b. Mesolithic period
   c. Neolithic period
2. Palaeolithic humans were ...
   a. nomads and farmers.
   b. nomads and hunter-gatherers.
   c. sedentary and livestock farmers.
3. Humans began to master fire in the ...
   a. Palaeolithic period.
   b. Mesolithic period.
   c. Neolithic period.
4. Humans began to bury the dead in ...
   a. the Palaeolithic period.
   b. the Mesolithic period.
   c. the Neolithic period.
5. In the Neolithic period, humans went from being ...
   a. farmers to livestock farmers.
   b. hunter-gatherers to producers.
   c. hunter-gatherers to consumers.
6. Pottery, basket-making and cloth are inventions from the ...
   a. Palaeolithic period.
   b. Mesolithic period.
   c. Neolithic period.
7. Prehistoric art reflects people's concerns about ...
   a. death.
   b. surviving the forces of nature.
   c. both a) and b).
8. The first metal that humans learned to work with was ...
   a. bronze.
   b. copper.
   c. tin.
9. Rock paintings were normally done ...
   a. inside deep caves.
   b. in only one colour.
   c. both a) and b).
10. The Venus of Willendorf represents ...
    a. an animal.
    b. a woman.
    c. a hunter.

02 Early civilisations

<< LOOKING BACK

- What marks the end of Prehistory and the beginning of History?
- Which continent is Egypt located on?
- What is a timeline?
- Can you name the longest river in Egypt?
- Where was writing invented?
- What do you call an Ancient Egyptian ruler?

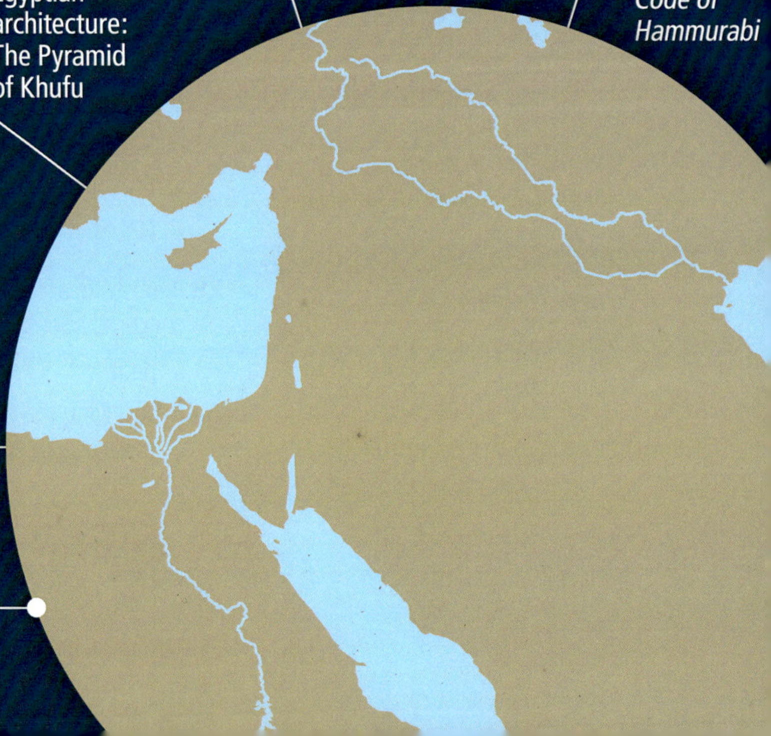

3500 BC
History begins

26th century BC
Sumerian art: *The Standard of Ur*

2585 BC
Egyptian architecture: The Pyramid of Khufu

2500 BC
Egyptian sculpture: *The Seated Scribe*

1756 BC
Babylonian sculpture: Stele of the *Code of Hammurabi*

Mesopotamia: the place where History began

Imagine a world without writing. 'Fantastic!', you might think. No homework, no exams … But before you start celebrating, think again. There would be no books, no newspapers and, of course, no internet, no e-mails and no instant messaging. Writing is so important to the development of civilisation that historians consider that History begins when writing first appeared in Mesopotamia around 3500 BC.

Early writing wasn't used to communicate great ideas, though. It was used to keep records and to count goods, materials and food. In fact, one of the first things that was recorded in writing was ale! Ale was the Mesopotamians' favourite drink and they used writing to record how much of it workers were given each day as part of their pay.

The earliest writing was just a series of marks scratched into clay tablets with a stylus made of reed, but it gradually evolved to become an early version of the writing we use today to record laws and communicate. So next time you use your 'stylus' to write on your hand-held 'tablet' computer, think about how much you owe the Mesopotamians and their ale.

?

- In what other ways would our lives be different today if we did not have writing?
- Do you think the way we write is changing today? How about in the way we send messages?

668 BC
Assyrian relief sculpture: *Dying Lioness*

5th century BC
Persian art: *Frieze of Archers*

LOOKING FORWARD >>

- Where did the first civilisations appear?
- What does the word *Mesopotamia* mean?
- What materials did the Mesopotamians use for building?
- What was the name of the Egyptian god of the dead?
- What were Egyptian pyramids used for?
- Which civilisation developed the first alphabet?

1 Early civilisations

Where did the first civilisations appear?

The first civilisations **appeared about 5 500 years ago in the Near East.** We know about these early civilisations because we have discovered **written** accounts from that period. These accounts have allowed us to learn a lot about the way people thought, what they believed in, what customs they held and how they lived. In this unit, we will focus on the civilisations in **Egypt** and **Mesopotamia**, and also learn about other civilisations around the Mediterranean.

WHAT IS A CIVILISATION?

A civilisation is an advanced state of human society in which there is:

- a stable food supply
- a division of labour
- a hierarchical society
- systems of law and government
- a developed culture

1.1 Economy and society

- These early civilisations began along the **banks of very long rivers**, such as the Nile in Egypt, and the Tigris and the Euphrates in Mesopotamia. These rivers crossed areas of desert, so people used their water to make the lands around them fertile for agriculture. They **developed irrigation systems**, such as canals and levees, to channel water to more distant areas.
- There was also a lot of **craftwork and trade** in the areas around these large rivers. In fact, so much trade took place that **people began to use money**.
- These early civilisations were **urban civilisations**. Economic activities were concentrated in **cities**. Some of these cities were home to political and administrative powers.
- **Society** in these early civilisations was very **hierarchical**. A minority, made up of kings and priests, controlled the majority of the wealth and governed the people. Under their command were the **army** and **civil servants**, who managed the kingdom. **Traders** were below these groups in the social hierarchy. Then came **artisans**, **peasants** and finally **slaves**.
- In ancient civilisations, the majority of labour was done by **slaves**. They were the **basis of the economy**. Slaves did not have rights and were considered to be the property of their masters.

MESOPOTAMIA AND EGYPT

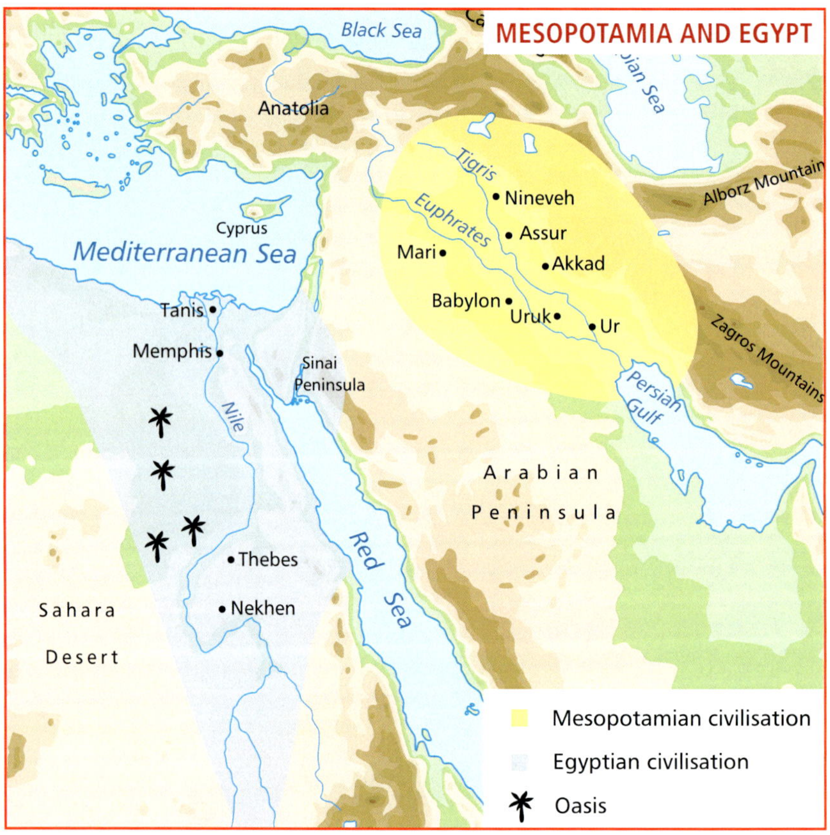

ACTIVITIES

1. Why did early civilisations appear near rivers?
2. Draw a pyramid to represent the different levels of society in early civilisations. Why do we say that society in early civilisations was hierarchical?
3. Why do you think advances in agriculture led to increased trade?
4. Find out the names of some early civilisations in South America and Central America.

1.2 Political structure

Early civilisations had **complex political structures**. Rulers imposed their authority on the rest of society by using **religious and military power**. They were all-powerful and acted as intermediaries to the gods. These rulers, especially the rulers of Egypt, identified themselves with the gods in order to justify their power. This led to the creation of the first dynasties of kings. Egyptian kings were known as **pharaohs**.

These kings surrounded themselves with royal officials who were in charge of collecting taxes, maintaining public order and enforcing laws. The first **codes**, or **sets of laws**, were written during this period. These codes regulated day-to-day life.

WARFARE

Warfare was also an important feature of these civilisations. Structured armies were created to defend borders, but also to invade and conquer neighbouring territories. These conquests led to the formation of the first empires.

A relief sculpture of Mesopotamian archers

1.3 Culture

One of the most important developments of these early civilisations was the appearance of writing. The earliest known example was **cuneiform writing**, dating from 5500 BC in Mesopotamia. Writing first came into existence as a way of keeping record of offerings made and taxes paid to temples. Therefore, the origin of writing is associated with religion and economic activities.

In **Mesopotamia**, writing was done by making wedge-shaped marks on a stone tablet with a stylus. This writing system is called **cuneiform writing**.

The **Ancient Egyptians** developed various systems of writing. The most complex one was **hieroglyphs**, which was based on elaborate drawings.

The people of these civilisations were **polytheistic**. This means they **worshipped various gods**. These gods represented elements of nature and other aspects of life, such as the Sun, the Moon, fertility, death, etc. **Temples** were built in honour of the gods, and were where elaborate ceremonies took place and sacrifices were made. These rituals were presided over by **priests** who acted as intermediaries between the people and the gods. Priests, therefore, had great influence in society.

SCRIBES

Scribes were those who learned to read and write. Usually only the sons of the wealthy could study to become a scribe, who would, in turn, be placed in a high position in society.

A relief sculpture of an Egyptian scribe

ACTIVITIES

5. What was slavery? What role did it have in society and the economies of early civilisations?
6. Which characteristics of early civilisations come from Prehistory and which began during this period?
7. What is your opinion on slavery? Do you think it is a thing of the past? Hold a class debate.

2 Mesopotamia

What does the word *Mesopotamia* mean?

Mesopotamia is a desert region crossed by the Tigris and the Euphrates. This is where History's first civilisations appeared some 5 500 years ago. The name *Mesopotamia* comes from the Greek for 'between two rivers'. The people of Mesopotamia channelled water from the two rivers and developed an economy of **irrigation-based agriculture**, which was the basis of their civilisation. Today, the territory of Mesopotamia corresponds to the countries Iraq, Kuwait and north-eastern Syria.

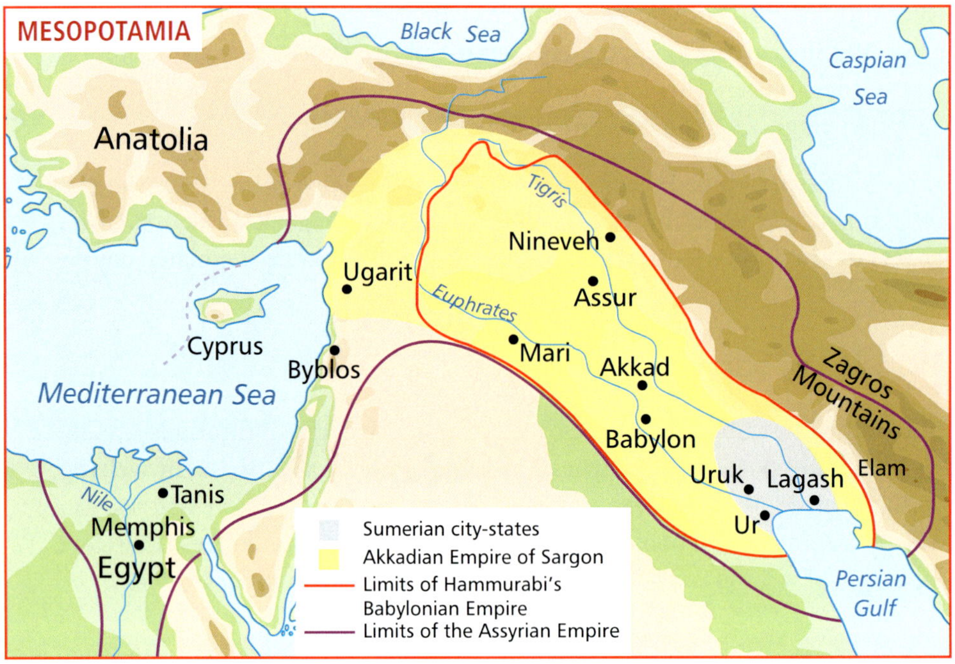

2.1 The history of Mesopotamia

Mesopotamia was home to four important civilisations: the Sumerians, Akkadians, Babylonians and Assyrians.

Sumerians

The Sumerians inhabited southern Mesopotamia around 3500 BC. They invented **cuneiform writing** and developed the first known civilisation. The Sumerians lived in **city-states**. These were independent cities with their own governments. At first, they were governed by priests. Later, they were ruled by kings with the help of priests. The most important city-states were **Ur**, **Uruk** and **Lagash**.

Akkadians

The Akkadians lived to the north of the Sumerians. They had a policy of expanding their territory to the south, into the territory of the Sumerians, which they eventually conquered. The conquest of Sumerian territory allowed **Sargon**, king of Akkad, to create the **first empire in History**. The Akkadians controlled the region from 2335–2150 BC.

Babylonians

Around 1950 BC, in the city of **Babylon** in the centre of Mesopotamia, there was a great royal dynasty. One of the most powerful kings of this dynasty was **Hammurabi** (1792–1750 BC). He held great power over Mesopotamia and introduced an important set of laws, the *Code of Hammurabi*, which was written in 1756 BC. This code of laws was used throughout his empire.

CODE OF HAMMURABI

The *Code of Hammurabi* is written on a stone stele divided into two parts. At the top is a depiction of Hammurabi, standing in front of the Sun god of Mesopotamia. Below are some of the code's articles:

'If anyone steals the property of a temple or of the court, he shall be put to death, and also anyone who receives the stolen thing from him shall be put to death.'

'If fire breaks out in a house, and someone who comes to put it out [...] takes the property of the owner of the house, he shall be thrown into that same fire.'

'If anyone steals the son of another, he shall be put to death.'

The *Code of Hammurabi*
Translation by L. W. King, 1898 (adapted)

Assyrians

The **Assyrians** lived in northern Mesopotamia. Their empire reached its peak between the 9th and 7th centuries BC. The Assyrians were fearsome **warriors** who developed advanced military techniques and were, therefore, able to create a great empire. Their most important cities were **Assur** and **Nineveh**, where the remains of a great library, the Royal Library of Ashurbanipal, have been found. There were also important palaces such as the palace of King Ashurbanipal.

DAILY LIFE IN MESOPOTAMIA

ACTIVITIES

8. Which modern-day countries are located in Ancient Mesopotamia?
9. Make a chart showing the different civilisations and empires of Mesopotamia in order from the oldest to the most recent.
10. Why do you think governments are usually located in cities?
11. The *Code of Hammurabi* was the first set of written laws in History. Is it important for laws to be written down? Why or why not?
12. Mesopotamia is considered to be 'the cradle of civilisation'. Find out what this means.
13. Research some other laws of the *Code of Hammurabi*. Do you think they were fair? Discuss.

3 Mesopotamian architecture, art and literature

What materials did the Mesopotamians use for building?

3.1 Mesopotamian architecture

The terrain of Mesopotamia is not very rocky, so the main building material used was bricks made of mud, or **mudbricks**. Very little Sumerian architecture has survived the test of time because mudbricks are much less resistant than stone. In Mesopotamian architecture, **semi-circular arches** and vaults were widely used.

To honour their gods, the Mesopotamians built temples called **ziggurats**, which were part of larger temple complexes. These were the most important buildings in Mesopotamian civilisations. They were immense structures in the form of stepped towers. Priests lived and performed religious ceremonies in them. Ziggurats were built by the Sumerians, Akkadians, Babylonians and Assyrians.

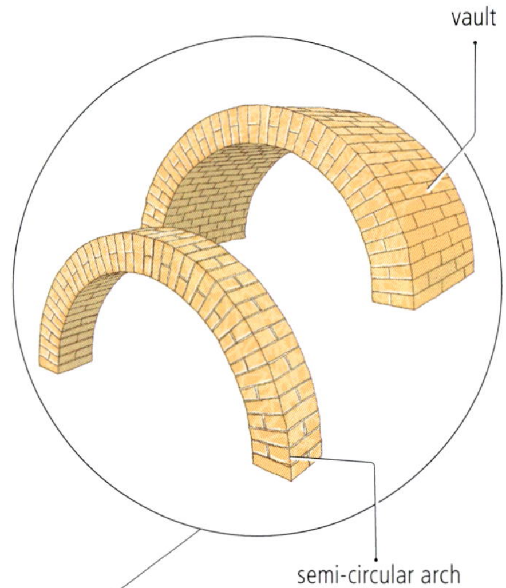

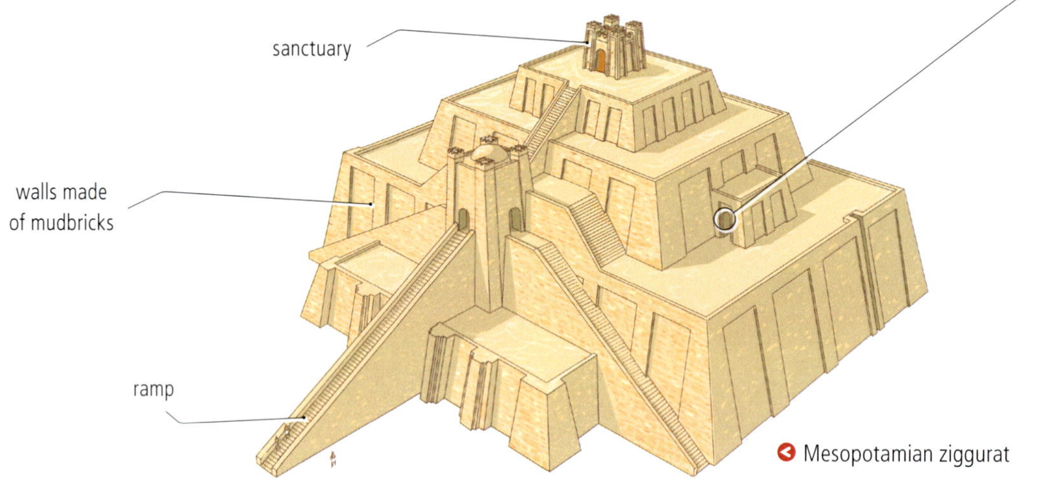

Mesopotamian ziggurat

3.2 Mesopotamian sculpture

Statues

Sumerian kings were intermediaries between the people and the gods. This is why Sumerian sculpture usually depicts them **praying**. In addition, Sumerian sculpture depicted people **disproportionately**, giving them large heads and small bodies. The figures are usually **seated** and have large eyes and inexpressive faces.

A statue of Gudea, ruler of the city-state of Lagash, from the late Sumerian period

ACTIVITIES

14. Draw a ziggurat and label the parts.
15. In your opinion, what is the reason for the lack of physical remains of Mesopotamian architecture?
16. Make an educated guess as to why ziggurats were tall.

Relief sculpture

Relief sculptures from Mesopotamian civilisations were sculpted on stone plaques, or on upright slabs of stone, called **steles**. Steles were placed in cities or temples to commemorate important events, such as a military victory. They depicted the gods and kings, often hunting or in battle.

The **warrior spirit** of the Assyrians is reflected in their art. The walls of their palaces were decorated with large friezes of battle and hunting scenes in relief. In Assyrian reliefs, the figures are very stiff and solemn. Figures were sometimes superimposed to give the scenes depth. Details, such as animal fur and horse harnesses, were sculpted very accurately.

Relief of the Assyrian King Ashurnasirpal II during a royal lion hunt

For a period following Hammurabi's reign, the city of Babylon was famous for **decorating the bricks** used in its structures, such as the Ishtar Gate.

THE ISHTAR GATE

The Ishtar Gate was the main entrance to the city of Babylon. It was built to honour the Babylonian goddess Ishtar. The gate was more than 12 metres tall and was decorated with brick reliefs representing young bulls (*aurochs*), lions, and dragons (*sirrush*).

A reconstruction of the Ishtar Gate in the Pergamon Museum, Berlin

A detail of a dragon on the Ishtar Gate reconstruction

3.3 Mesopotamian literature

As we already know, writing developed in Mesopotamia as a way of recording payments, offerings and taxes brought to temples. But did you know that the **first great work of literature** was written by the Sumerians? The ***Epic of Gilgamesh*** was an epic poem about Gilgamesh, the king of the Mesopotamian city-state Uruk. The poem is written on 12 tablets. We know about the poem today as some tablets have survived.

Enheduanna was an Akkadian princess and the daughter of Sargon the Great. Sargon appointed her as high priestess of the Moon god, Nanna, in the most important temple in Ur. She held great political power, but is best known for what she wrote. Many literary and historical scholars consider her to be the earliest author and poet that we know by name. Two hymns written by her in Sumerian cuneiform have been discovered.

What was an Akkadian princess doing in Ur anyway?

ACTIVITIES

17. What are the differences between Sumerian sculpture and Assyrian reliefs?

18. Look at the Ishtar Gate. Apart from honouring the gods, what other reasons could there be to build such an impressive monument as a city entrance?

19. Why do you think the clay tablets of the *Epic of Gilgamesh* survived but most Mesopotamian architecture did not? Discuss with your classmates.

4 Egypt

What was the name of the Egyptian god of the dead?

The civilisation of Ancient Egypt developed over a period of 3 000 years. Its history is divided into three periods, or **kingdoms**, and two intermediate periods when they were invaded. After the last empire, Ancient Egypt went into decline.

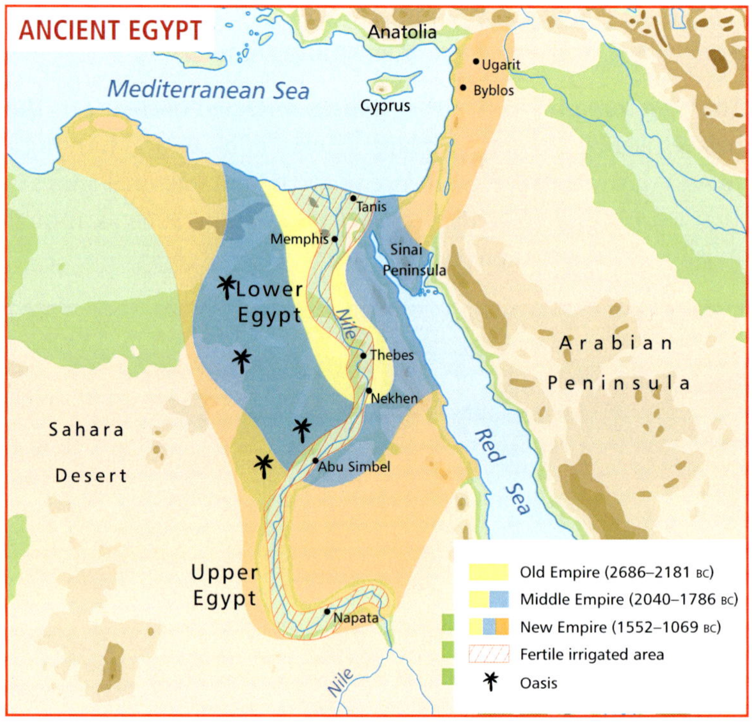

4.1 Society in Ancient Egypt

The **pharaoh** was the most powerful person in Ancient Egypt. He was the **political and religious leader** of the Egyptians, and was considered to be the incarnation **of the god Horus**. As political leader, he also owned all the land, made laws, collected taxes and was the head of the military.

As religious leader, he performed rituals and built temples to honour the gods. The pharaoh had a court of **priests** and **scribes**, who were civil servants with a knowledge of hieroglyphic writing. The priests supervised the worshipping of the gods at the **temples**, which were also economic centres that collected offerings and taxes from the common people.

4.2 Religion in Ancient Egypt

Egyptian religion was **polytheistic**. Their many gods varied in their relationships to one another, depending on the period and area.

The Egyptians were very interested in **death**. They believed that the souls of the dead travelled to the afterlife to be judged by Osiris, the god of death and resurrection. Therefore, their bodies had to be kept in good condition. This led to the development of **mummification**. They also buried the dead with the *Book of the Dead*, which contained prayers that would allow them to pass the judgement of Osiris.

THE GODS OF ANCIENT EGYPT

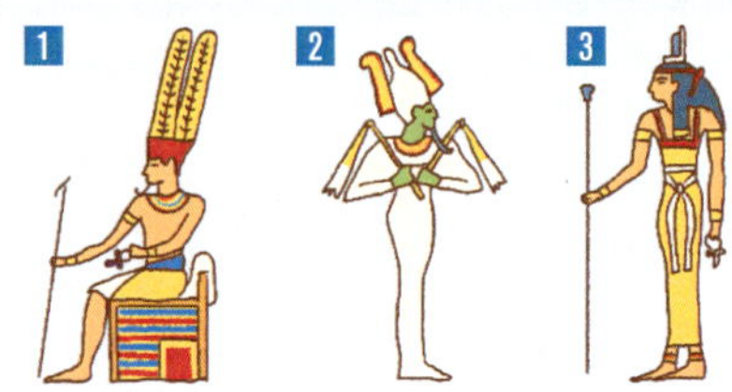

1. **Amun-Ra** was the god of the Sun and the official god of the pharaohs.
2. **Osiris** was the god of death and resurrection.
3. **Isis** was the goddess of motherhood. She was the wife of Osiris and queen of the gods.

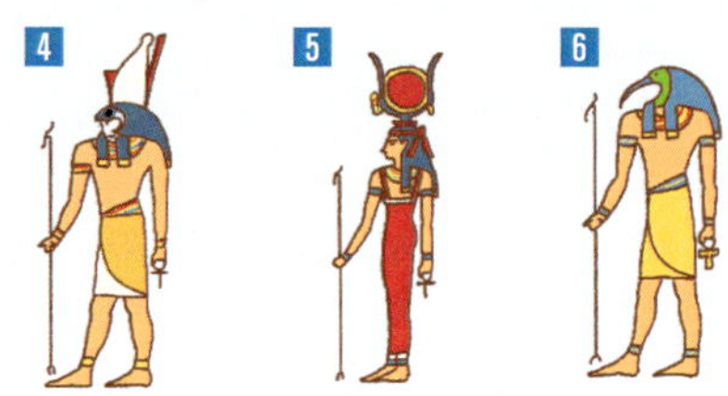

4. **Horus** was the son of Isis and Osiris. He was the protector of pharaohs.
5. **Hathor** was the wife of Horus and the goddess of love and joy.
6. **Thoth** was the god of wisdom.

ACTIVITIES

20. Write definitions for the following terms: *pharaoh, scribe, priest, polytheism.*
21. Answer the questions:
    a. According to the Ancient Egyptians, what happened to them when they died?
    b. Why were bodies mummified?
22. Look at the information about the gods of Ancient Egypt on the right. What does the worship of gods like these tell you about Egyptian society?

4.3 The Nile River and Ancient Egypt

The Ancient Egyptians considered the **Nile River** to be the father of their kingdom. The river overflowed every year and the fields along its banks flooded, leaving behind mud that was very good fertiliser for crops. Harvests were plentiful and **agriculture was the basis of the economy.** This agricultural wealth allowed cities, craft and trade to develop, as Egypt needed to obtain wood and metals in exchange for its crops.

The flooding forced Egyptians to develop certain areas of **knowledge**, such as **astronomy**, **geometry**, **arithmetic** and **engineering**.

ACTIVITIES

23. Did temples serve only as religious buildings in Ancient Egypt?
24. Why were Egyptians buried with the *Book of the Dead*?
25. Find out why the god Hapi was so important to the Egyptians.

5 Egyptian architecture and art

What were Egyptian pyramids used for?

Egyptian art and architecture were dedicated to the pharaoh and the gods. For this reason, it was **solemn**, **monumental** and **very large**.

As a child, **Howard Carter** was fascinated by Ancient Egypt. At the age of 17, he began archaeological work in Egypt. In 1922, he discovered the stunning collection of treasures in the tomb of Pharaoh Tutankhamun.

What do you think the curse of the pharaoh is?

5.1 Tombs

The tombs built by Ancient Egyptians reflected **how important death was** to them. The tombs in which pharaohs were buried were complex structures, intended to preserve the body and surround it with wealth for its journey to the afterlife. There were many **burial chambers** inside the tombs, which were **decorated with paintings and inscriptions**. There were various types of tombs, such as mastabas, pyramids and hypogea.

Mastabas were a single underground chamber covered by a truncated pyramid.

Pyramids were made up of one or many surface-level chambers.

Hypogea were underground tombs carved into the rock, with various chambers.

5.2 Temples

Egyptian temples were very large structures, built to honour the gods. Only **priests**, **scribes** and **servants** worked in temples, as these buildings were not intended for public use. Ceremonies were performed outside the temple, so their **exterior** was **spectacular**, with obelisks and long avenues of sphinxes. Two of the most important temples are in **Luxor** and **Karnak**.

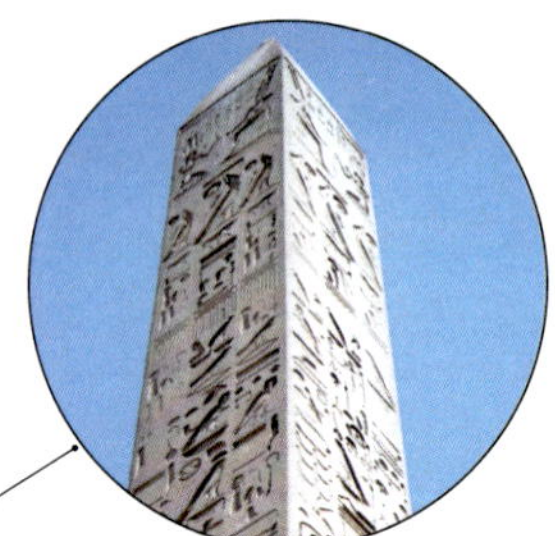

5.3 Sculpture

Egyptian sculpture evolved very little over thousands of years because its purpose did not change. Its purpose was to represent the gods and pharaohs, and to communicate **distance** and **solemnity**. We can identify some common characteristics of Egyptian sculpture:

Sculpture of Pharaoh Menkaure with goddesses

ART DURING THE REIGN OF AKHENATEN

Pharaoh Akhenaten ruled Egypt from 1372 to 1354 BC. During his reign he implemented many political and religious reforms. There were also changes in artistic expression and the repetitive figure of the pharaoh disappeared. Instead, royalty were depicted much more realistically, as you can see in this sculpture of Akhenaten's wife, Nefertiti.

5.4 Painting

Egyptian **painting** depicted a wide variety of subjects. In addition to religious and royal subjects, there were scenes of daily life, such as dancing, farming and bread-making. Human figures were represented according to certain rules: the head and extremities were seen in profile and the torso was shown face on.

A painting from the tomb of Kenamun

ACTIVITIES

26. Compare the sculptures of Menkaure and Nefertiti on this page and note down the differences.
27. Make a list of the characteristics of Egyptian sculpture.
28. Hypogea were built to hide royal tombs. Why would the Ancient Egyptians want to do this?
29. Think about what you learned about pharaohs on page 34 and read section 5.1 again. Why would workers be happy to help build pyramids for their rulers?
30. Why do you think historians consider Egyptian paintings to be primary sources?
31. Find out who the Ancient Egyptian Imhotep was. How is he related to the Pyramid of Djoser?

6 Other early civilisations

Which civilisation developed the first alphabet?

6.1 The Phoenicians

The Phoenicians lived in **city-states** on the coast of modern-day Lebanon. Due to the coastal location of Phoenicia and the abundance of wood for building ships, the Phoenicians became the **greatest sailors** and navigators in the Mediterranean.

The Phoenicians controlled Mediterranean **trade routes** between the 12th and 8th centuries BC. They travelled as far as the British Isles in search of goods and circumnavigated the African continent in around 600 BC. They established trading colonies throughout the Mediterranean, including Carthage. They also made an extremely important contribution to culture, the **alphabetic writing** system, which they spread throughout the Mediterranean and the Near East.

CARTHAGE

Carthage was a Phoenician colony on the north coast of Africa and one of the greatest cities in the Ancient World. The Phoenicians chose the location because it was sheltered, easy to defend and there was an abundant supply of fish.

The ruins of Carthage

6.2 The Hebrews

For a long time, the Hebrews were nomads and were dominated by other cultures, such as the Egyptians. However, the Hebrews created the Kingdom of Israel between 1010 and 932 BC. The main rulers of this kingdom were Saul, David and Solomon. After a brief period, the Hebrews were again subjugated, but this time by the Assyrians and the Babylonians.

Their religion, **Judaism**, was **monotheistic**. In other words, they believed in one god. Their god was called **Jehovah** and their holy book was the **Torah**. The Torah was very influential on later religions, including Christianity, because the Torah forms part of the Old Testament of the Bible.

DID YOU KNOW?

The name *Phoenicia* comes from the Greek for 'land of purple'. This is because the Phoenicians were the first to use and trade a dye called Tyrian purple, which did not fade easily.

Why do you think dye was such a valuable product in the Ancient World?

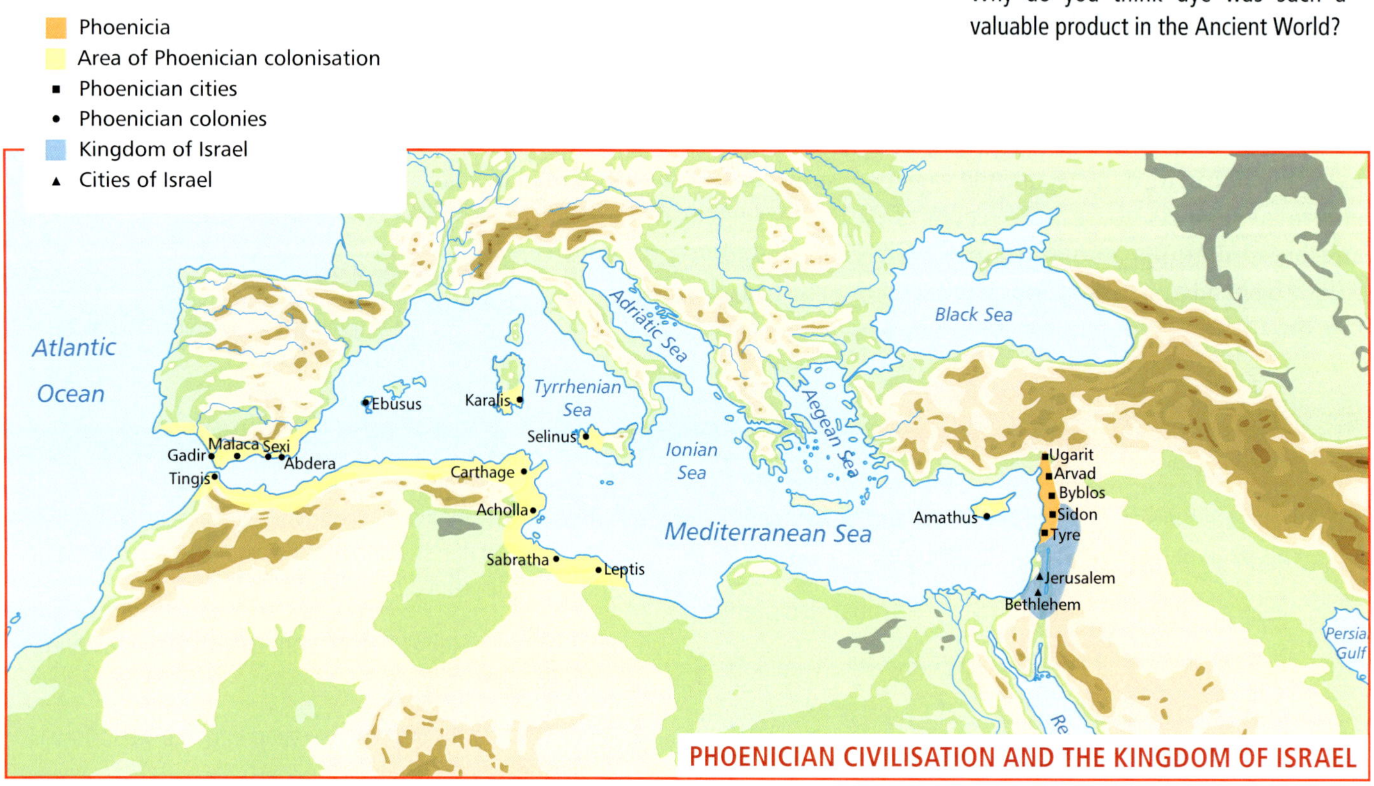

PHOENICIAN CIVILISATION AND THE KINGDOM OF ISRAEL

6.3 The Persian Empire

The Persians were native to the **Iranian Plateau**. They created an empire which reached its peak between the 6th and 4th centuries BC. It included modern-day Iran, Mesopotamia, Egypt and the Anatolian peninsula.

The empire was powerful and successful because:

- It was a **centralised empire** under the command of an absolute king, a 'king of kings'. The most important kings were Cyrus the Great, Cambyses II and Darius the Great.
- Although it was enormous, the empire had an excellent **system of roads** and, consequently, the postal service and powerful army could move quickly from place to place.
- The territory was divided into provinces, or **satrapies**. They were ruled by governors, called **satraps**. Civil servants, known as the 'eyes and ears of the king', kept close watch of the satraps to prevent any attempt to become independent.

Persian art and architecture

The purpose of Persian art was to emphasise the splendour of the king's court. Remains of large palaces at Pasargadae, Susa and Persepolis have survived. The Persians used both architraves and vaults in their buildings.

THE PERSIAN EMPIRE

Origin of the Persian civilisation
Persian Empire of Cyrus the Great
Persian Empire of Cambyses II
Persian Empire of Darius the Great
• Major cities of the Persian Empire
Gandhara Satraps

PERSEPOLIS

Darius the Great built the most impressive palace in Persepolis, the Apadana Palace. It served as the location for some of the complex ceremonies which characterised the Persian court and which emphasised the power of the 'king of kings'.

The apadana was the most important room in the palace. It was a large hall with columns, used for official ceremonies.

The palace walls were decorated with relief and ceramic sculptures of processions of soldiers armed with lances and bows and arrows.

ACTIVITIES

32. Explain why the Phoenicians were such good sailors and navigators.
33. What was the Phoenicians' most important contribution to culture?
34. What was unique about Judaism? How does it differ from the religions of the Ancient Egyptians and Mesopotamians?
35. List the three main characteristics of the Persian Empire.
36. Find out who destroyed the Apadana Palace at Persepolis. What did its destruction coincide with?
37. Hold a class debate. Discuss which is more important to us today: the Phoenicians' development of an alphabetic writing system or the Sumerian cuneiform writing system?

Discovery techniques

TIMELINES

Analysing a timeline

Timelines allow us to represent a succession of events over time in a visual way, using a line labelled with dates and information.

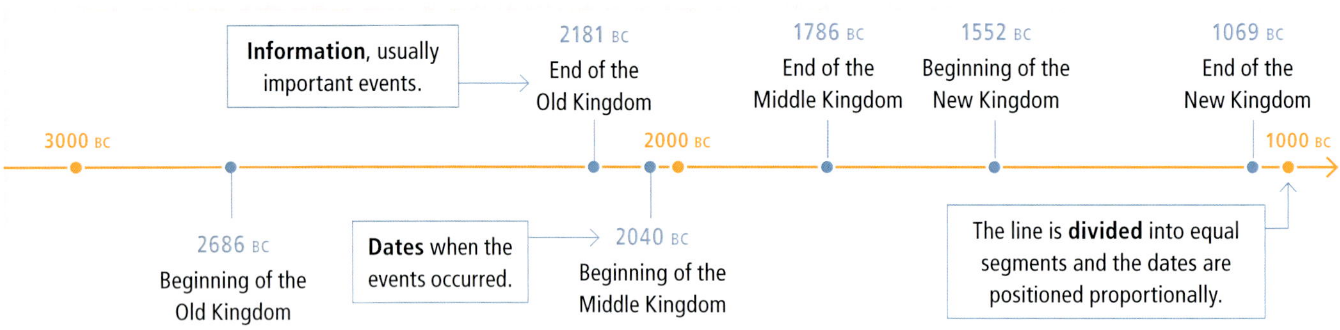

Making a timeline

1. Analyse the information and the dates you are going to use. We are going to include the following events:
   - Construction of the Pyramid of Khufu completed (2560 BC)
   - Beginning of the Akkadian Empire (2335 BC)
   - Reforms of Amenhotep IV (1372–1354 BC)
   - Beginning of the reign of Assyrian King Ashurnasirpal II (883 BC)
   - *Code of Hammurabi* (written 1756 BC)
   - End of the New Kingdom in Egypt (1069 BC)
2. Put the events in chronological order, from the oldest to the most recent.
3. Draw a straight line and divide it into segments, e.g. one centimetre equals 100 years.
4. Position the dates of the events in the correct place and label it with the corresponding event.

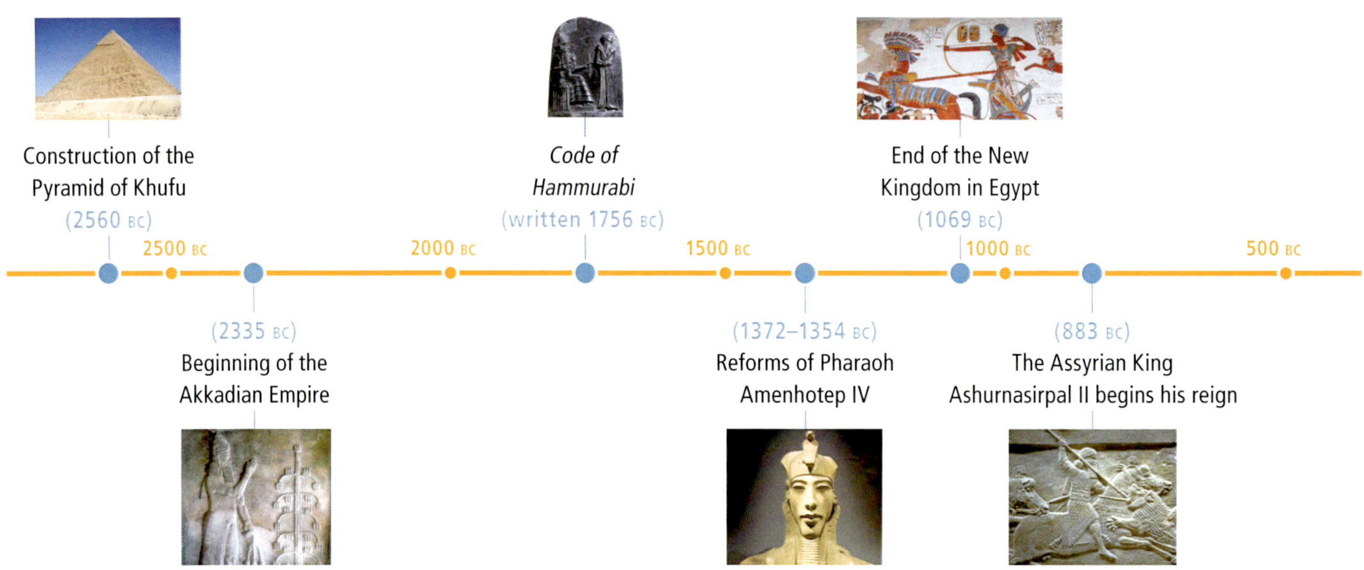

Comparing timelines

We can approach the chronological study of various historical processes in two ways:

- **Diachronically**: looking at the evolution of a set of events from the oldest to the most recent.
- **Synchronically**: studying several processes at the same time so that we can compare them.

The timeline we created earlier gathered information about the history of two different civilisations. It was a diachronic timeline of the history of early civilisations.

However, with the information on this timeline, we can, for example, do a synchronic study of the history of Egypt and Mesopotamia. This enables us to look at what was happening in different civilisations at the same time.

Construction of the Pyramid of Khufu (2560 BC)

Reforms of Pharaoh Amenhotep IV (1372–1354 BC)

End of the New Kingdom in Egypt (1069 BC)

2500 BC — 2000 BC — 1500 BC — 1000 BC — 500 BC

Beginning of the Akkadian Empire (2335 BC)

Code of Hammurabi (written 1756 BC)

The Assyrian King Ashurnasirpal II begins his reign (883 BC)

2500 BC — 2000 BC — 1500 BC — 1000 BC — 500 BC

ACTIVITIES

1. Make a timeline of the rulers of Ancient Egypt. Include information about the three kingdoms and these rulers:
   - Djoser (2670)
   - Hatshepsut (1479)
   - Senusret III (1878)
   - Mentuhotep II (2040)
   - Khufu (2589)
   - Ramesses II (1279)
   - Sobekhotep VI (1719)
   - Pepi II (2278)
   - Akhenaten (1353)
2. Make a timeline showing the most important events in the life of a member of your family.
3. Make a diachronic timeline of your life and then make a synchronic timeline with one of your classmates.

Revision activities

1 Copy or trace this map in your notebook:

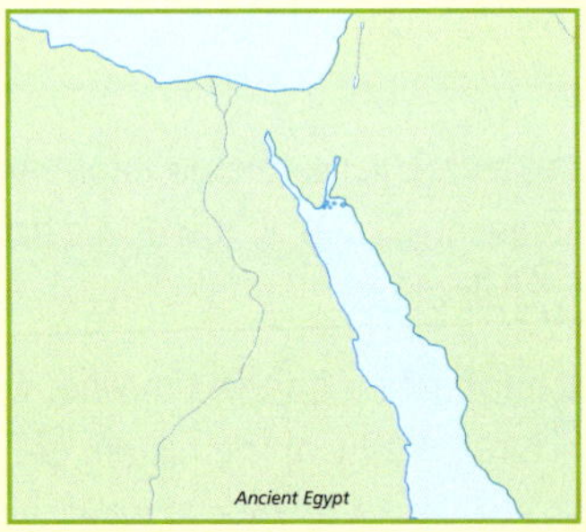

a. Label the following: *Nile River, Nile Delta, Upper Egypt, Lower Egypt, Mediterranean Sea, Red Sea, desert* (twice).

b. Colour the fertile areas in green, the river and other bodies of water in blue, and the desert areas in yellow.

c. Mark the location of the main cities in Ancient Egypt with a red cross.

d. Based on your knowledge of Ancient Egyptian civilisation and reflecting on this map, answer these questions:

- Why would people say that Ancient Egypt was 'the gift of the Nile'?
- How could a desert serve as a natural protective barrier against potential enemies?
- How can location and trade contribute to a city's prosperity and power?
- Compare this map with the one on page 34. What do you think were the major problems of keeping such a large empire running smoothly?

2 The Greek Herodotus is often referred to as 'the father of History'. After his trip to Egypt, he wrote the following account of the construction of pyramids. Read it and then answer the questions:

> "Khufu [...] commanded that all the Egyptians work for him. So some were commanded to extract stones from the stone-quarries in the Arabian mountains and to carry them across the Nile. Others he ordered to receive the stones after they had been carried across the river in boats, and to take them to the Libyan mountains. There worked 100 000 men at a time, each man for three months continually. For the making of the pyramid itself there passed a period of 20 years [...]. It is built of stone, smoothed and fitted together in the most perfect manner. [...] On the pyramid it is declared in Egyptian writing how much was spent on radishes and onions and leeks for the workmen, and that [...] a sum of 1 600 talents of silver was spent."

- What do you think was Herodotus' general impression of the construction work on the pyramid?
- How does the construction of pyramids prove that there was a division of labour in Egypt? Give evidence from the text.
- What is the relationship between the existence of a strong government and the carrying out of these monumental projects?

3 King Tutankhamun was a pharaoh of the 18th dynasty in the New Kingdom. He died very young and was buried in the Valley of the Kings. His tomb was discovered almost intact in 1922 by Howard Carter. It was the most complete royal tomb ever found. Below you can see Tutankhamun's sarcophagus and two artefacts found in his tomb.

a. As a primary source, what kind of information can the tomb and these objects provide?

b. Why do you think this discovery was so important to the study of Ancient Egypt?

4 Define these terms: *civilisation, city-state, empire, polytheism, social hierarchy, scribe, pharaoh, dynasty, pyramid, afterlife, monotheism, Torah, satrapies, apadana.*

5 Use a Venn diagram to compare and contrast early civilisations in Egypt and Mesopotamia. Mention characteristics that are unique to each one and also those that are shared by both. Try to include information on location, the system of government and religion.

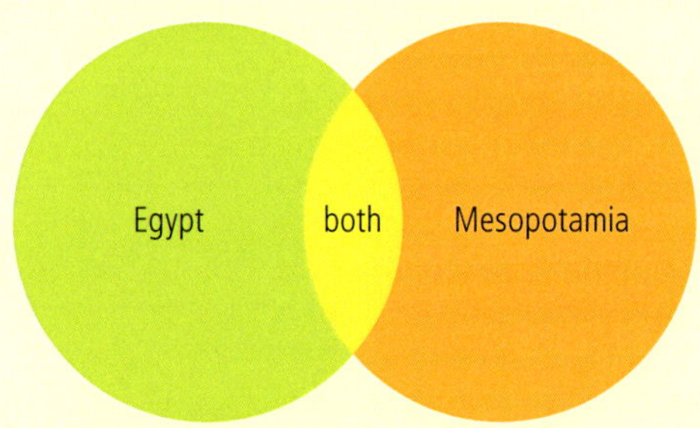

6. In pairs, look at the words in orange circles in the spider diagram. They are aspects present in a civilisation.

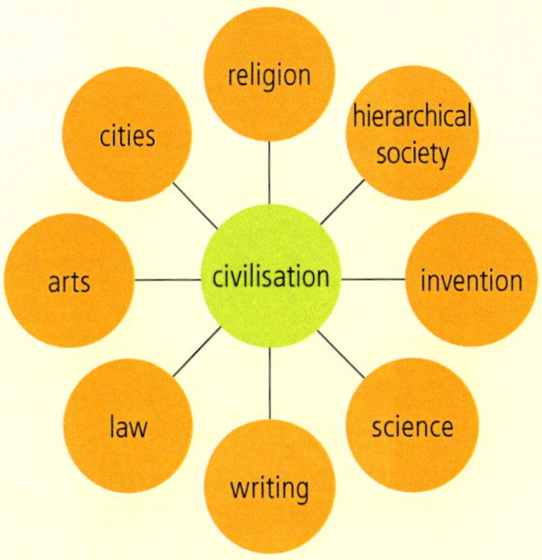

Now read these six words: *architecture, farming, temple, slavery, trade, water.* Choose three to complete the diagram.

a. Which of the resulting 11 words can be associated with government? Explain your answer.
b. Which word must have come first in order of time and which one do you think came last? Discuss. Then, share your answer with the whole class.

7. Complete this chart about architecture in Mesopotamia and Egypt:

	MESOPOTAMIA	EGYPT
Materials		
Architectural elements		
Representative buildings		
Function		

8. Answer the following questions:

a. Why do we say that History begins with the invention of writing?
b. Why were scribes important to the societies of early civilisations?
c. The only buildings that have survived from early civilisations are temples and tombs. What conclusions can you make from this fact?
d. Would you say there is a distinction between politics and religion in early civilisations? Why or why not?
e. Do you think religion plays an important role in public life today? Explain your answer.

9. Create a guide to an early civilisation. Choose between Mesopotamia and Egypt, and make a brochure or pamphlet with information about your chosen subject. Include information on daily life, religion and major accomplishments. Use the internet or reference books to help you. Illustrate your guide with drawings and maps.

10. Draw like an Ancient Egyptian. Draw a self-portrait using the Egyptian painting style. Follow these simple steps:

a. Draw the head in profile and the eye from a front view. You can also draw a black wig!
b. The shoulders and torso are shown from the front.
c. The hips, legs and feet are drawn in profile.
d. Outline everything in black and colour in the skin.
e. Men wore short skirts and women wore straight dresses. Their clothes were usually white.

11. Make a mummy. Learn about the process of mummification with this simple experiment. You will need an apple, plastic cups, baking soda, salt and weighing scales.

a. Slice the apple in two. Weigh both pieces and write down the results. Place each half into a plastic cup.
b. Carefully mix ½ cup of baking soda and ½ cup of salt and pour it over one of the halves, completely covering it.
c. Put both slices of apple in a dark and dry place (e.g. a cupboard) for a week.
d. After a week, take the apple slices out and remove the salt and baking soda. What do you observe? Weigh the two slices again. Compare the results and draw conclusions.

What have you learned about mummification from this experiment?

12. There was a large number of gods and goddesses in Ancient Egypt and they varied from place to place and from period to period. Some estimates suggest there were over 2 000 different deities worshipped in Ancient Egypt. The **pantheon of Egyptian gods** is the name we give to the 'family tree' of Egyptian deities. Do some research and design your own pantheon of Egyptian gods. You can draw it in your notebook or make a slide presentation on a computer. Compare your pantheon with your classmates'. There will definitely be some differences!

Read and think

HIEROGLYPHS

Hieroglyphs are the 'characters' of a system of picture writing called **hieroglyphic script**, which was created by the Ancient Egyptians approximately 5 000 years ago. At first, hieroglyphs were pictures of objects, or **pictograms**, that the Egyptians wanted to represent. Later, these pictograms also often represented an idea. These signs are known as **ideograms**. Then, they also started to represent one or more **consonant sounds**. Therefore, Egyptian hieroglyphs were a combination of sound signs, pictograms and ideograms. When Egyptian hieroglyphs were first discovered, scientists obviously found them almost impossible to understand. It was made even more complicated because the vowel sounds were not represented and, in addition, the Egyptians wrote horizontally, vertically, from left to right and from right to left!

Scribes were responsible for writing hieroglyphs, but it took them a long time to write anything, especially as they often had to write on stone. So, in time, they invented a new form of writing called **Demotic script**. This was faster and easier to write.

Hundreds of years later, archaeologists discovered hieroglyphic writing on the walls of Egyptian pyramids and tombs. Although lots of archaeologists could read Demotic script, no one knew the meanings of the old hieroglyphs.

Then, about 200 years ago, a stone tablet was found in Egypt. This stone, now called the **Rosetta Stone**, had a story written on it in Greek, Demotic script and hieroglyphic script. As many archaeologists could read Greek and Demotic, they could begin to read hieroglyphs. But even today, it is still difficult to interpret hieroglyphic scripts accurately.

Egyptian hieroglyphs at the Temple of Isis in Philae

The Rosetta Stone

ACTIVITIES

1. True or false? Correct the false statements.
   a. The Ancient Egyptians were not the first people to use hieroglyphic script.
   b. All hieroglyphs are pictograms.
   c. The problem with writing in hieroglyphs was that it was very slow.
   d. There were hieroglyphs on Egyptian pyramids and tombs.
   e. Archaeologists started to read hieroglyphs about 500 years ago.
2. Answer the questions.
   a. What type of sounds were represented by hieroglyphs?
   b. Why is it complicated to understand hieroglyphs?
   c. Why was the discovery of the Rosetta Stone so important?
3. Why do you think hieroglyphs are so important to historians?
4. Use the chart on the right to do the following activities:
   a. Write the following words in hieroglyphics: *pharaoh, Nile, pyramid, god.* Check your answers with a partner.
   b. In what situations might you use hieroglyphs instead of normal writing?
   c. Work in pairs. Write a message in hieroglyphs to your partner. Do you understand your partner's message?

Work it out

CONCEPT MAP

Use the words in the word cloud to create your own unit map in your notebook. Write any connecting texts you need.

Old Kingdom
New Kingdom
Babylonians
social hierarchy
developed culture
Sumerians
Mesopotamia
laws
Akkadians
Early civilisations
first written record
division of labour
characteristics
Middle Kingdom
Assyrians
Egypt
polytheistic
government
irrigation-based economy

SELF-ASSESSMENT

Carry out a self-assessment of what you have learnt in this unit. Choose one answer for each question and then check your answers.

1. Mesopotamia was a desert region between the rivers ...
   a. Tigris and Nile.
   b. Nile and Euphrates.
   c. Tigris and Euphrates.
2. Writing in Mesopotamia was ...
   a. hieroglyphic.
   b. cuneiform.
   c. demotic.
3. The first empire in History was formed by ...
   a. Hammurabi.
   b. Sargon.
   c. Ur.
4. Sumerian city-states were first governed by ...
   a. kings.
   b. soldiers.
   c. priests.
5. Ziggurats were Mesopotamian ...
   a. vaults.
   b. temples.
   c. sculptures.
6. Assyrian friezes showed ...
   a. battles.
   b. daily activities.
   c. buildings.
7. The Egyptian Sun god was called ...
   a. Isis.
   b. Amun-Ra.
   c. Horus.
8. Sphinxes were ...
   a. temples.
   b. priests.
   c. sculptures.
9. Which of the following statements about Egyptian sculpture is false?
   a. People's faces were inexpressive.
   b. Their heads appeared in profile.
   c. The figures were symmetrical.
10. Enormous monoliths with a pyramid shape at the top were called ...
    a. pylons.
    b. obelisks.
    c. lintels.

Glossary

A

Account (n): a written or spoken description of an event

Adobe (n): a mixture of earth and straw made into bricks and dried in the sun, used to build houses in some parts of the world

Afterlife (n): the life that some people believe begins after death

Alloy (n): a metal that is made by mixing two or more metals, or a metal and another substance

Amulet (n): an object worn because it is believed to protect against evil, disease or unhappiness

Architrave (n): CLASSICAL ARCHITECTURE a lintel which lies across the tops of columns, specifically the lower third entablature

Arise (v): to occur or begin to occur because something else occurs

C

Carrion (n): dead or decomposing flesh

Carving (n): an object or a design made by cutting stone or wood

A carved bison made of reindeer antler

Circumnavigate (v): to sail all the way around something, for example, the Earth or a continent

D

Development (n): a new event that changes a situation

Dye (n): a substance used to change the colour of something

Piles of dye in a modern market

Dynasty (n): a series of rulers or leaders who are all from the same family or a period when a country is ruled by them

E

Edible (adj): can be eaten without making you sick

Embed (v): to fix something firmly into a substance

F

Flourish (v): to grow well or be successful

Frieze (n): a narrow piece of decoration along a wall, either inside a room or on the outside of a building just under the roof

G

Gather around (v): come together around something or someone

Genus (n): BIOLOGY a taxonomic group for classifying living things that is above species and below family

H

Harness (n): a set of leather bands placed around the body of a horse or other animal that connects it to a vehicle

Hierarchical (adj): arranged in order of status or importance

Human evolution (n): the process by which modern humans developed from primates over a very long period of time

I

Incarnation (n): the physical form of a god or divine entity

L

Lintel (n): a horizontal piece of stone or wood which supports the wall at the top of a door or window

An Egyptian tomb

M

Mine (v): to dig coal or another substance out of the ground

Mould (n): a shaped container that is used to make something in a particular shape, by pouring a liquid into it which later becomes solid

O

Order (n): BIOLOGY one of the main taxonomic groups; it comes above family, genus and species

Ore (n): rock or soil from which metal can be obtained

P

Peak (n): The point of highest activity, quality or achievement

Peat bog (n): an area of soil that is made up of decaying plants. The soil can be used as a fuel

Prey (n): an animal that is hunted by another animal for food

Profile (n): a side view of a person's face

This Egyptian scribe is depicted in profile

R

Reign (n): the period of time when a king or queen rules a country

Roasting (n): the technique of cooking something in an oven or over an open fire

Fish roasting on an open fire

S

Schematic (adj): showing only the main form and features of something, usually in the form of a drawing

Schematic rock painting

Sedentary (adj): staying in one place; not moving from one area to another

Shelter (n): a place that is protected from bad weather or danger

Slab (n): a large, thick, flat piece of stone or wood

Species (n): BIOLOGY the smallest of the main taxonomic groups, coming after genus

Sphinx (n): an ancient imaginary creature with a lion's body and a human head

Stele (n): ARCHAEOLOGY an upright stone slab with an inscription or relief sculpture

The stele of the *Code of Hammurabi*

Stiff (adj): rigid, not flexible

Subjugate (v): to defeat people or a country and rule them in a way that allows them no freedom

Superimpose (v): to put a picture, words, etc., on top of something else

Surplus (n): an amount of something that is more than what is required

T

Thatch (n): straw or reeds used to make roofs

A hut with a thatched roof

Transition (n): a change from one situation to another

Truncated (adj): made shorter by removing the top or an end

Mastabas are like truncated pyramids

U

Undergo (v): to experience something, especially a change

V

Vault (n): a roof made up of an arch or a series of arches

A vaulted room

W

Warfare (n): the activity of fighting a war

Big thinkers

Name: Richard Leakey

Lived: 1944–present day

Nationality: Kenyan

Interests: Politics, paleoanthropology

Bright ideas: He conducted important paleontological research on several expeditions. In 1967, Richard formed the Kenya Museum Associates (now Kenya Museum Society). He also founded WildlifeDirect in 2005 to conserve African wildlife and endangered species.

Name: Howard Carter

Lived: 1874–1939

Nationality: British

Interests: Archaeology, Egyptology

Bright ideas: He was known for developing archaeological methods for protecting excavation sites. He discovered the tomb of Pharaoh Tutankhamun in 1922. When he retired from archaeology, he became a part-time agent for collectors and museums.

Name: Enheduanna

Lived: 2285–2250 BC

Nationality: Akkadian

Interests: Politics, poetry and hymns

Bright ideas: She was the daughter of King Sargon and a high priestess. She held great political power, but is best known for what she wrote. She left behind hymns and dedications to the goddess Inanna written in Sumerian cuneiform. Many literary and historical scholars consider her to be the earliest-known author and poet.